HITTING SECRETS OF THE PROS

Big-League Sluggers Reveal the Tricks of Their Trade

WAYNE STEWART

McGraw·Hill

New York   Chicago   San Francisco   Lisbon   London   Madrid   Mexico City
Milan   New Delhi   San Juan   Seoul   Singapore   Sydney   Toronto

1 2 3 4 5 6 7 8 9 0   AGM/AGM   3 2 1 0 9 8 7 6 5 4

ISBN 0-07-141824-5

McGraw-Hill books are available at special quantity discounts to use as premiums and sales promotions, or for use in corporate training programs. For more information, please write to the Director of Special Sales, Professional Publishing, McGraw-Hill, Two Penn Plaza, New York, NY 10121-2298. Or contact your local bookstore.

This book is printed on acid-free paper.

To my wife, Nancy, and my sons, Sean and Scott

Contents

Acknowledgments

First and foremost, thanks to my editor, Mark Weinstein, who once again came up with a great idea. This time it was for a series of books on inside tips and information straight from the source—big-league players, coaches, and managers. The two books thus far are on hitting secrets and on pitching insights. Clearly, without him these books would never have come to fruition.

Second, it was great talking baseball and working with Editorial Team Leader Craig Bolt. It really helps to work with folks who know publishing as well as baseball, and that's been the case with Mark and now Craig.

Finally, a big thanks to the pros themselves, especially those who went way beyond merely giving me a few quick answers to my queries: Ken Griffey Sr. and Jr., Rudy Jaramillo, Ryan Klesko, Lee Smith, Trevor Hoffman, Merv Rettenmund, Billy Wagner, Jeff Bagwell, Craig Biggio, Johnny Damon, Scott Stewart, Jim Thome, Willie Upshaw, Eric Byrnes (and his father, Jim), Terry Francona, Rickey Henderson, Luis Gonzalez, Kent Tekulve, Duane Espy, Tom McCraw, Dr. Charles Maher of the Indians; along with the media departments of many clubs, especially the Cleveland Indians, the San Francisco Giants (particularly Bobby Evans), the Anaheim Angels, and the Arizona Diamondbacks (with a special thanks to Susan Webner).

Also, thanks to Gray & Co. for giving me permission to use material from *Indians on the Game*, a book that I did for them a few years back.

Foreword

OVER THE YEARS I've learned how to put a program together that suits the swing of today, or from way back. When I was in the minor leagues starting back in 1983, I was always into hitting. Even before that, when I was in Rookie League, I was a coach and started working with hitters. That's what I wanted to do in the Rangers' organization, and I was fortunate enough to become the minor-league hitting instructor. At that point I was a symptoms coach. For example, I might tell one player, "Hey, you're getting out front. Your head's coming out. You're going around the ball. You don't have good balance."

Those are all negatives, and, in fact, I've already given the guy four or five things to think about. In hitting you're supposed to see the ball and hit the ball, and I was trying to get this guy to think about too many things at once.

Eventually, when I got into the big leagues, I remember the guys at that level said, "We want it as simple as one-two-three." I studied the films and so forth, and I figured that I had to get at the root problems that underlie all those symptoms. What I developed is what we use here in the Rangers' organization throughout the system.

The fundamentals when a hitter is in a good hitting position have never changed, even since the days of Babe Ruth. Hitters did the same things then that they today do mechanically to get into a good hitting position, to recognize pitch and location, and then to trust their eyes to tell their hands whether to react or not. So it's a really simple philosophy that we use here.

Obviously, one of the most important things is you've got to see the ball. Second, you've got to have a rhythm. Third, you need separation—that is, as your front foot is going forward, your hands are going back. Like a rubber band, you're getting into what Charlie Lau used to call a launching position, a power position. Fourth, you have to stay closed. That is, you have to stay inside the doorjamb, inside the door, staying square, closed, not flying open early, so you can let the ball travel longer. The longer you're closed, the easier it is to stay inside the ball and through it. Fifth is the weight shift—so you're back, letting the ball get to you, and you recognize the pitch; then you shift into it.

The hard part is putting those five things together and timing the pitcher. But it's simple because you can always fall back to how to fix yourself.

The longer you can let the ball get to you and still hit it out front, the better you'll be. We always say, "Stay back until you're ready to attack it." That way we can get recognition, see if it's a strike or not; then the path to the ball is going to be there because of staying closed, of staying inside, and going through the ball.

The great hitters have good timing and great eyes—and great hand-eye coordination. For them the mental factors are the bottom line—whether they can deal with the mental part of this game.

The fundamentals are just one part—something we do day in and day out. We hit early every day, doing drills for the muscle memory. The preparation is important, but once the game starts, you need to study what the pitcher does in different situations—his velocity and pitch selection—and develop a plan. Then you need to go to the plate trusting in that plan and execute it.

If you're trusting your plan, your breathing is really slow and your mind is clear. That's something that we work on because if your mind is cluttered, it's going to distract you from seeing the ball and affect your timing. You'll be thinking about things like "Where are my hands?" or "I've got to get my foot down." You get into trouble when you're not trusting yourself. If you've prepared adequately and built up your muscle memory, you don't even have to think where your hands are; you're trained.

Visualization should also be a big part of a hitter's preparation. Good hitters visualize success. The night before a game, we get together in our clubhouse to watch films of the pitcher. When you do that, you can see what his fastball does, his breaking ball, his change-up, and then you can prepare that night or the next day because you've already seen that image of what the ball does. When you come to the park for the game, you're already prepared. You've already visualized what you want to do and how you're going to attack this pitcher.

Actually, I don't rely that much on watching game films to coach my hitters because my eyes are trained to see what I need to see every at-bat. Often I look at game films just to confirm what I've seen a hitter do in practice. Most of the time I'm right because I know what I'm looking for. I know my hitters, and I know the fundamentals they should be using in their swing. My eyes tell me if there's a problem.

You have to learn your hitters so you know who you can correct during a game and who you should talk to later. Each hitter is unique. Some guys want you to approach them right then, some guys come to you and ask, "Hey, what'd you see?" and other guys run up to the video room right after the game and watch their swings. I just have to adjust to each hitter. I can't tell them, "Do it this way," because it feels good to me. It may not feel good to them, and they're the ones who are hitting. They have a lot of pressure on them day in and day out while they're playing, on top of the traveling and so forth.

So I have to adjust to them. For example, if a hitter has two strikes, I tell him to do what feels comfortable to him, whether it's choking up, spreading his feet out, thinking of going the other way, or being a little more aggressive in the zone. If he doesn't have success, then *he* needs to make an adjustment.

There are no real mysteries to hitting. You need to figure out what suits each hitter, the proper mechanics. I just try to make them aware of what they're doing when they're successful versus when they're not. Good hitters need to have a feel, and a rhythm, and a trigger that allows them to have good timing.

— RUDY JARAMILLO
HITTING COACH, TEXAS RANGERS

1

Hitters' Styles

BABE RUTH, Ted Williams, Stan Musial, Hank Aaron—these men all had style. However, there are vast differences in players' styles.

It boils down to a simple phrase: "Whatever it takes." Those words typify the thinking of many major-league hitters—they'll do whatever it takes to succeed. From scrutiny to cheating and with many stops in between, hitters strive to make it to the major leagues and, once there, to stay there.

One of the most vital factors hitters consider—of which the average fan is oblivious—is the count on the hitter. Start with the 0-0 count. There are two prevailing styles for leadoff hitters. One is the player who starts the game looking for a first-pitch fastball. He wants to tee off on it, get a hit, perhaps a homer, and disrupt the game. A single and a stolen base for a speed burner such as a Johnny Damon or a Rickey Henderson can be effective as can a leadoff homer from a player like Henderson, who had the speed-power blend, or from Brady Anderson in his peak year of 1996.

Other tacticians hold to the idea of lying back for a while. They may take a pitch or two, see what the pitcher's got, make him expend some energy, and work him deep in the count to learn his speed, thinking, and approach that day.

Damon, who has hit leadoff most of his career, said, "It's different at certain times. Yeah, you want to be able to jump on a fastball, but—guess what—if you make an out on the first pitch, well, no one really knows how the pitcher's curveball is that day or if he's throwing his change-up. So, I actually like to go out there and work the count. But sometimes I go up there swinging."

As a rule, it sounds as if he prefers to employ the tactics of his former team. He said, "I still have the Oakland A's approach—wear the pitcher down so he doesn't have good stuff and then you can get to the bullpen and wear down the bullpen so your team is in better shape for the following days."

He explained the trickle-down, or domino, effect: "The next starter has to pitch more innings because the bullpen is shot. So, that's my type of philosophy—work the count and do some damage that way."

By way of contrast, Damon said Henderson hit many of his leadoff homers using the first-pitch fastball approach. "Pitchers definitely did not want to fall behind Rickey and possibly walk him, so they would try to get that first pitch over, and Rickey would be ready for it. That's why he has that record [for career leadoff homers]."

All-time hit king Pete Rose did not like the idea of swinging at the first pitch. Sure, if he knew the pitcher was likely to groove a first-pitch fastball, Rose would not be averse to taking a cut, but he felt that hitters who have a habit of attacking the first offering give pitchers an advantage. In high school, where pitchers' control is rather shaky, it's great to sit on fastballs. However, major-league pitchers are so skilled, they'll toy with a hitter who constantly chases first pitches.

By taking the first pitch against a pitcher on a given day, a batter might accomplish several things, including avoiding a futile stroll back to the bench after a quick at-bat. That not only helps out the pitcher, but also saddles the batter with a quick 0 for 1 on the young day. In addition, by waiting things out, the hitter can take a good look at this pitcher: his release point, the type of speed he has that day, and the break on his ball.

Rose felt that what worked best for him when leading off the game was to go after the 1-0 pitch. Most pitchers throw a fastball in that situation, not wanting to open the game down 2-0. In the latter case, the pitcher would then most certainly have to offer up a fastball.

Clearly, Henderson, recognized as best leadoff hitter ever, performed his leadoff role differently than Rose. Henderson said that he does like to look for, and then drive, first-pitch fastballs. He estimated that of all his record-setting leadoff homers (to start contests, not just innings) "probably 40 percent of them [came using that tactic]. When I first started off, knowing that I could hit home runs, Bobby Bonds [the former record holder for leadoff homers] taught me the first thing [to do] when you go up to the plate [is to] 'zone' it [look for a pitch in a specific area], take a hard swing at it, and if you make contact, you might hit the ball out of the ballpark. If you don't make contact, you put fear in the pitcher. So it always made sense [to try that style of hitting] and sometimes I connected," he said with a laugh and more than a touch of understatement.

If pitchers came to realize what he was doing, why didn't they throw him a breaking ball or a junk pitch or even a waste pitch on the game's first pitch? He replied, "They did, but, see, I had so many different weapons, if they threw an off-speed pitch, a curve, and it wasn't in the strike zone, then they get behind in the count and they end up walking me—so I was more of a threat on the bases." Pitchers found themselves in a no-win situation against Henderson.

Despite the multitude of Henderson's leadoff blasts, he said he would and did "work the count, but sometimes they were so much in fear that I would be on the base paths [with a walk], that they said, 'I gotta get ahead of the guy and quick.'" This would cause them to try and get ahead 0-1 to Henderson, to be in a spot where they were on top and could, as Henderson put it "work his pitches, so I started adjusting to the game. Then, when they tried to get ahead of me, I tried to zone them up, and if they threw pitches in my zone, I used to take a whack at it."

Even if Henderson hadn't accumulated tons of leadoff homers, he still would have been a force in that lineup slot. He drew more walks, scored more runs, and stole more bases than any player in baseball history. He attributes such success to "being patient, also being able to hit with two strikes. I think you have to be comfortable hitting with two strikes as a leadoff hitter."

In 2002, as a Boston teammate of Henderson, Damon got to observe the all-time great up close. "I think Rickey was just blessed. I mean, he was blessed with a great eye. And Rickey is very confident—Rickey's confident in Rickey.

"When he came around, there wasn't anybody like him. He definitely was a trendsetter, and he's what teams are looking for in a leadoff hitter. Before [him], leadoff hitters were just slap hitters and guys who could run very fast, but Rickey added the power to that game." His speed and stolen bases were a huge plus, and, as Damon commented, before Henderson it seemed like "the power was never involved. That's why you're seeing guys like myself and Darin Erstad and Ray Durham evolve into leadoff hitters, because we do have some sock in our bats, we do know how to work counts, and we, for the most part, have gotten the job done throughout our careers."

He illustrated how big the influence of a leadoff hitter can be, "When I'm going good, it's fun and exciting for our team." Often, to paraphrase an old political expression, as the leadoff hitter goes, so goes the team.

Damon feels Henderson was unique in that he stayed in the leadoff spot for an eternity. "I see myself moving in the batting order as my career progresses. I think I might have 11 or 12 [leadoff home runs] right now. But I do take a lot of pitches, even if the first pitch is right down the middle. But that's my game and I feel like I can help my team be a better team on that certain day." In Damon's case, through 2002, he could only recall three of his leadoff homers coming off the game's very first pitch.

When a game's leadoff hitter comes to the plate later in the game, he still leads off innings a significant number of times, but not always. Sometimes, then, his role changes. For instance, after a National League pitcher has made an out and jogs back to the bench with, say, two outs and nobody on base, the leadoff hitter has a little-known, secondary job to perform. He takes on a new style of hitting for such at-bats.

He stalls. He leaves the on-deck circle looking like Mickey Rivers on an especially slow day, almost hobbling to the plate. Once there, he steps out and elaborately looks to his third-base coach as if there would be a play in this situation. All he's doing, of course, is giving his pitcher, who is about to labor again on the hill (perhaps during a scorching day in Texas or St. Louis), a "blow," as basketball players call such a short rest.

Damon pointed out that playing in the American League, with the designated hitter rule, he doesn't have to worry about such histrionics. "You hit in this league," he said. "Yeah, they have great hitters over there [in the National League], but the main object is home runs over here; over there, there's a lot more strategy involved."

Hitters delight when they bat with a hitter's count such as 2-0 or 3-1. Reliever Billy Wagner said with a chuckle that the hitters who excel in such situations include "about everybody in the league, I guess. I mean, there should [still] be baseball etiquette that you can throw a 3-0 pitch right down the middle and the hitter'll take it. Nowadays, you got so many young kids that don't know the etiquette of the old guys, that you don't throw a 3-0 pitch down the middle unless you've really got a great fastball or a great slider or something."

Many great hitters such as big Frank Thomas were so skilled because, in part, they ate up pitchers' mistake pitches the way a glutton puts a hurt on an All-You-Can-Eat buffet bar. Known also as "cripple hitters," men like Thomas thrived when a pitcher threw, for example, a delectable fastball in a curveball situation.

A young hitter, though, should learn that, while he may have been given the green light to hit on a 3-0 count in high school where he was the stud, in the majors managers like Sparky Anderson will often have them strategically take a pitch.

In theory, a young hitter feels, "Hey, why not hack at a 3-0 pitch? The pitcher is gonna groove me a fastball." Maybe so, but a veteran realizes that even if he gets his pitch, he may hit it hard, but right at somebody for an easy out. After all, even when a hitter puts the ball in play, there is no guarantee it will find a hole. If that were the case, there would be many more .400 hitters out there. So, sometimes a hitter is wise to take a pitch, do nothing, and yet still help the team by perhaps drawing a walk. After all, even if he takes a strike, the pitcher still has to throw another one on 3-1.

A smart hitter is geared to take a cut at a 3-1 offering. The hitter works the count, makes the pitcher get behind, and now the payoff is, most likely, a good pitch to tear away at. That is especially true if the pitcher has begun to struggle with his control. If a pitcher has worked deep into the game and now seems to have lost his control, the odds are he won't suddenly find his groove again. The smart bet is to assume he will continue to struggle and either make a mistake pitch or continue to throw balls, not strikes. By extension, a smart hitter knows that such a pitcher, especially when behind in the count, will *have to* throw fastballs, the pitch most hitters love to face.

Part of baseball's cat-and-mouse game in which hitters and pitchers try to "toy" with one another, is a trick some veteran hitters achieve when they set up a pitcher. Usually fans think in terms of the pitcher being in control, setting up a hitter for a pitch that will retire him, but it can work the other way around as well.

Early in a game between the Milwaukee Brewers and the Cleveland Indians toward the tail end of his career, slugger Hank Aaron purposely looked bad on a Jim Kern pitch. Aaron knew that later Kern, then a youngster, would go back to that same "baffling" pitch in a more important situation. The wily Aaron was right, and later that game he came up with a key hit off Kern.

More recently, hard-hitting Mo Vaughn mentioned three men good at working the pitcher. He said, "The offensive game is definitely a cat-and-mouse game. Barry Bonds is one of the best at this. Albert Belle and Manny Ramirez are good at it, too."

According to Vaughn, a batter might take a pitch early in a game "when you know you can drive it to set the pitcher up. Later, in a more important [at-bat], you'll get that pitch again." In other words, the pitcher gets lulled into serving up that juicy pitch again. This time a man like Ramirez will crush it.

Along those same lines, in his famous book *The Science of Hitting*, Ted Williams wrote that he loved getting a second chance at a pitcher after he had retired Williams on a pitch he felt had fooled "The Splendid Splinter." "I couldn't *wait* to get up again, because I knew he would throw it again." And when he did, Ted was ready to make the pitcher pay the price.

Many coaches tell their players to think and act differently when the count goes to two strikes. One approach to two-strike hitting is to look for a pitch on the outside corner while trying to react if the ball is inside. Some say the hitter should ideally be thinking: just make contact, put the ball in play or at least foul it off—just don't strike out.

Rod Carew was a man who had hits flowing off his bat the way fruit flows from a cornucopia. According to a *Baseball Digest* article, he feels hitters are actually fearful of hitting "with two strikes. That's why they don't work the count more. It's an insecurity thing. They might get that one pitch they can drive, and they're afraid they might not see it again in that at-bat. So they want to make sure they take advantage of it."

In the same article, Walt Weiss told writer Jim Armstrong, "It's not real comfortable hitting with two strikes. Guys don't like to get deep in the count because it takes away their aggressiveness if they get a strike or two on them."

A study of the 1999 season revealed Weiss had a good point. Big-league hitters owned a .338 batting average for their at-bats when they hit the first pitch, but hit a meager .192 when they had two strikes on them. Plus, they would hit a homer every 24.1 at-bats off the first pitch versus only one home run every 49.6 at-bats on two-strike counts.

Williams said when he had two strikes on him, he did change his thinking—he'd forget about hitting homers and would even shorten up on the bat as he tried to have the bat head meet the ball. Unfortunately, today's mentality dictates that home runs are king and striking out holds no shame, an attitude much different than that of the early days of the game.

Then again, some hitters are effective even with two strikes. Wagner said, "I think the [best] one that I've seen is Wade Boggs. There was a guy who you had a hard time striking out. Some hitters have said they're comfortable at 2-2. [My attitude is], '2-2? Hey, now I can throw you anything.' But some guys like having two strikes: they protect and they concentrate a little more."

Several umpires openly admitted they had a different strike zone for men such as Boggs. Ron Luciano confessed, "If Rod Carew has two strikes on him and fouls off five pitches and then takes the sixth down the middle, I'm calling it a ball." Years earlier, umpire Bill Klem was working the plate when rookie pitcher Johnny Sain faced Rogers Hornsby. Sain complained when three borderline pitches were all called balls. Klem retorted, "Young man, when you pitch a strike, Mr. Hornsby will let you know."

A more modern version of that tale comes from all-time saves king Lee Smith, a man who didn't gripe about the double standards. "I had one time in my life I asked an umpire about a pitch. That was when I was facing Willie Stargell of Pittsburgh, and I threw three fastballs, *right there*, and I was 3-0," he laughed. "And I ended up getting him to pop the ball up. I asked the umpire, 'Excuse me, ump, was that outside?' He said, 'If it was a strike, he would've swung at it.'

"Stargell was pretty much at the end of his career, but I'm telling you, imagine him in his prime: you throw it out there [on the outside part of the plate] and he hit the ball to the opposite field, to the warning track." So, Stargell could take an outside pitch and have it called a ball if he chose to do so, or he could take a whack on it and produce, at the very least, a sacrifice fly if that is what he needed to do.

Batters all know the counts where they would be wise to look for breaking balls: typically, 0-2, 1-2, and, with some pitchers or in certain game situations (e.g., with men on scoring position with first base open), even 3-2.

Conversely, most big-league hitters tend to sit on fastballs with counts of 1-0, 2-0, 3-0, 3-1, and, as discussed in cases such as Rickey Henderson's, with no count on the hitter.

Since many hitters, not just leadoff men, often love to attack the first tasty pitch they encounter, usually a fastball, it's become a baseball version of love at first sight. Jose Macias noted, "Like every hitter, I like fastballs." However, aside from that given, different hitters also like pitches in certain locations. Some players are, for example, great high-ball hitters.

He says that while he clearly does have a favorite pitch, he's crafty enough not to reveal what it is. "If I say it now, everybody is going to find out, and later they won't give me that pitch." He also said that hitters hope a pitcher makes a mistake and gives him "his pitch—leaves it right there." When that happens, batters hop on it and usually hit it hard.

Some hitters, like Jesus Alou, Vladimir Guerrero, or Yogi Berra (who said he loved high pitches) say that every pitch is their favorite pitch. To paraphrase Will Rogers, they never met a pitch they didn't like. Such players are known as having wide strike zones and are labeled "bad ball hitters."

Macias, a former teammate of the aggressive-hitting Guerrero, stated, "He likes everything and he can [hit everything]. I saw him hit a [bad ball] that almost hit the ground, and he hit a home run." In effect, said Macias, Guerrero has no strike zone: "Everything they throw [that's] close, he's going to swing at it and he can get it."

It's true. Guerrero attacks everything. In 2002 he told *Baseball Digest* that he had always been able "to not have a strike zone. I go to swing. When the pitch comes, I don't have to get a pitch down the middle. If I like the pitch, even if it's 15 inches off the plate and that's the pitch I wanted, I'm swinging."

Clyde King had a free swinger when he managed Atlanta. "Some hitters," said King, "try and hit the ball where it's pitched. Ralph Garr hits the ball *if* it's pitched."

The 2002 Twins made it to the ALCS before bowing out. They had hit .272 as a team that season but could muster only a .217 average in the ALCS versus the Angels. The free-swinging Twins had no homers and scored just seven runs in the four-game set. The reason seemed to be that they chased after pitches instead of working the count. Falling behind, they fared poorly.

Twins first baseman Doug Mientkiewicz opined, "We had too many guys who wanted to be the hero every time they stepped up to the plate. We didn't get here by hitting home runs. We got here by playing small ball."

As far as individual styles, superstar Tony Gwynn, a complex batter for pitchers to solve, had a relatively simple style of hitting. Not only did he perfect a swing that led to thousands of hits being deposited into the opposite field, but he always knew exactly why he was doing what he did.

For instance, even when it came to timing his swing, Gwynn had it down to a science. He said he honed his swing in on the 80- to 85-mile-per-hour fastball. Like another great hitter, Stan Musial, Gwynn looked for such pitches but was quick to change when necessary.

His thinking on hitting was nearly flawless. As he said back in 1992, keeping things simple was his secret. "I use a basic approach: never change," he stated succinctly. Clearly, for him, such a technique was perfect.

Rose's theory on trying to hit the baseball as hard as possible is a bit like the old line used by beginning pool players when they see a heap of their balls to shoot at, but aren't experienced enough to observe a good shot. Often they'll simply, "H H and H," that is, hit hard and hope. In baseball it sometimes pays off to hit the ball hard, hoping it finds a hole and doesn't become an "atom ball" (hit right at 'em) for a hard out.

In fact, former big leaguer Gus Bell once told his grandsons, now professional players, to be sure that they were swinging the bat hard. Woodie Held agreed, coming up with a colorful quote, "Don't forget to swing hard in case you hit the ball." Even the great Babe Ruth went along with such thinking. He said when he went for home runs he would "swing as hard as I can, and I try to swing right through the ball." He indicated he tried to follow through the same way a prizefighter did. He continued, "I swing big, with everything I've got. I hit big or I miss big."

Likewise, outfielder Dave Parker's hitting philosophy was far from cerebral. He once offered, "My approach is: see something I like and attack it." His words pretty much reiterate one of baseball's oldest sayings: "See the ball, hit the ball." That terse piece of advice is as far away from Williams's tenets as the theory of evolution is from the concept of babies coming from storks. It does seem strange, then, that the science of hitting, often so complicated, can ironically, at times, be reduced to such a simple formula.

Solid line-drive hitter Rico Carty, for one, often succeeded by simply looking for a pitch he could handle and then hitting it hard. And don't forget, Carty was one of those hitters that made managers utter in awe, "He could get up in the middle of winter and drill a line-drive double off the wall."

Former batting champ Andres Galarraga explained his approach to hitting: "The first thing I try to do is make hard contact—not hit home runs, just go for line drives." However, powerful Andre Dawson once said of Galarraga, "He's a guy who you can make a mistake with him, and he'll lose the ball."

Some hitters take the power tack, using what's basically a swing-from-the-heels approach, others stress hitting for contact. When a power hitter can also hit for average while avoiding the occupational hazard of sluggers—strikeouts—he is truly special. Yankee legend Joe DiMaggio had the best ratio of home runs to strikeouts ever. He had a remarkable ratio of nearly one homer for each of his times striking out (361 home runs to

369 whiffs). Some other players heading this list of power prowess coupled with good contact were Hall of Famers Berra, Williams, and Musial.

Bonds, another complete power hitter, drew 151 more walks than strikeouts in 2002. The only other man to walk 100 or more times over his strikeout total for an entire season was Williams, and he did this five times. Not only that, Bonds fanned only 47 times in '02 while collecting 46 homers, good for a DiMaggio-like ratio.

In contrast, Hall of Famer Wee Willie Keeler said his style of hitting was all about finding holes in the defense. His exact quote on the subject was, "Keep your eye clear and hit 'em where they ain't." It doesn't come much simpler than that.

Perhaps contact hitter Joe Sewell did manage to simplify the act of hitting to an even more rudimentary level when he created the adage, "You have to keep your eye on the ball." If anyone knew how true that advice was, it was Sewell. From 1925 through 1928 he struck out only 30 times; in 1930 and 1932 he struck out six times, just three times in each of those seasons. Further, he set an all-time record by going 115 straight games without a single strikeout.

Different hitters like to position themselves at various spots in the batter's box. Hall of Famer George Brett, for instance, liked to stand deep in the box, giving him longer to wait on the pitch. Harry "The Hat" Walker, a great hitting coach, advocated such an approach, having his hitters wait to see "what the ball is going to do." In other words, he felt players should see the ball and then react to it.

However, catcher Tom Lampkin said that few hitters change their spot in the batter's box in order to adjust to, or try to take, something such as a curveball away from an enemy pitcher. Still, he observed, "I would say that there is some of that [shifting in the box] at this level. I'm very aware of where people are in the box as a catcher, and I know that people have said that they'll position themselves in the box to take away certain pitches, but I've never [done that]. I'm not that good, I guess. I always stand in the same spot and I have a concept of the strike zone where I am now and if I start moving around in the box, then my concept of the strike zone changes."

Lampkin said that those batters who do move around in the box feel that it definitely helps them. Against a pitcher with a big curve, the strategy is to move up in the box to get to the ball before it has a chance to bend. Versus a hurler with a good fastball, logic dictates the hitter move back as far away from the pitcher as possible, deep in the box. This supposedly allows the fastball to slow down just a bit, thus offering the hitter a slight advantage.

Some hitters, says Lampkin, might make such a move hoping that the catcher tries to cross him up, hoping that the pitcher will see him deep in the box anticipating a fastball, and instead throw a curve. His actual intentions are to set the defense up, as he is really geared up for the curve now. "There are some smart hitters out there," he contended.

In fact, he said that two secrets of second baseman Roberto Alomar's success are his baseball savvy and duplicity. "He's a guy who moves around in the box a little bit, but you never know what he's thinking. He might be doing it because he knows that I watch, and he might be waiting for a certain pitch." As a result of Alomar's study of the game, he has been, to borrow a line from sportswriter Bob August, "as steady as a metronome."

Macias said that he, as a reserve, has a definite approach to the game, one that is somewhat different from that of the regulars. "I keep myself ready to play. Every day I work out, and some times I [come in for] early hitting. And when I don't play, I go in the batting cage to swing and get ready for whenever they need me late in the game.

"When I take my batting practice, I keep my hands 'inside' the ball and hit the ball where I want to—direct the ball when I hit it." He works on little things, too, like his concentration, adding that throughout all his practice his coaches "give me a lot of help and it works for me." That way, he said, "When I go in the game, I don't think about it. I just go in there, concentrate, see the ball, and keep my hands inside. It's little things, but most of the things that keep me sharp are [things like] going in the batting cage to get extra swings."

The ultimate challenge of coming off the bench is the pinch-hitting role. One of the all-time masters of this art was Smoky Burgess. In the book *Pen Men* by Bob Cairns, Burgess shared some of his secrets. First of all, his style was to focus on the enemy pitcher. Then he'd select a player from his own team who, like himself, hit left-handed. At that point, he'd study how the pitcher, in various situations, worked that left-handed hitter. When Burgess was later called upon to hit, he'd base his guesses on what pitches he'd get upon how the pitcher had worked that teammate earlier.

Cleveland Indians broadcaster Matt Underwood said it is pretty obvious that not everyone can be an effective pinch hitter. "First of all, there are some guys who just cannot sit; they've got to play everyday. We had Geronimo Berroa here a couple of years ago. Because he has so much movement in his swing, he's not the kind of guy who can sit for a long time and come off the bench and try to get a hit every now and then. Certain guys just have to play to maintain their swing.

"Then there are other guys who have what we call 'low-maintenance swings,' and they're great pinch hitters. I thought Bill Selby was great in that role because he has a short stroke, quick to the ball. I think he also has the right mental approach. I remember talking to him about it, and he said, 'It's a role that you have to prepare for every day. You have to watch the game closely, and, when the game gets into the late innings, you have to look at the lineup and at who's pitching and know you might get called on in a specific spot. You must be ready to get called on.'

"You can't say, 'Oh, geez, I gotta' pinch hit?' and grab a bat and run up there. The good players prepare from the first pitch to the last out to get in there at some point. They start looking for their spot; the guys who follow the game and really study it can almost pick their spot and think right along with the manager so they're not surprised when they get called upon to pinch-hit.

"It's also knowing your role—that you're not an everyday player, so you're not going to be disappointed when you come to the park and you're not in the lineup—that's part of it, too. There are some guys who are very good at that," he concluded.

It helps, too, if the hitter can figure out who, based on the tendencies of the opposing manager, he is most likely to face and what pitches he is likely to see.

Hard-hitting Richie Sexson added his theory on why some guys don't pinch-hit well. "Some guys are routine oriented—everybody on the team has a certain job that they have to do, and they become accustomed to it. Obviously [a guy like] Hank Aaron was never a pinch hitter in his life [actually, rarely: 17 for 87 (.195)], and when it came time to do it, he probably couldn't do it because he wasn't used to it. He didn't have a routine for it; he had no idea how to go about it.

"I think when you're kind of a career pinch hitter, a guy who doesn't play every day, you get into a routine and a rhythm in order to fit into your role." Sexson feels that a big part of hitting is being comfortable; hitters thrown into a pinch-hitting role who aren't used to it don't exude confidence or feel as if they can do the job well—therefore, they don't do well.

One common thread to the great pinch hitters is their philosophy that if a pitch looks good, they will be ready to take their hacks—especially since that may be the only good offering they get for that at-bat, and by extension, for the entire game.

Standout hitting instructor Merv Rettenmund feels that the art of pinch hitting is essentially fastball hitting. He should know. Through 2002, he said he believes he still holds the San Diego team record for the most pinch-hit appearances in one season. "You have to be on a really bad club to establish that record. And I was. I was on a club where I could pinch-hit for about everyone." In 1977, as a Padre, he was 21 for 67 (.313) as a pinch hitter, leading the league in both departments.

"So, you go up 100 times in one season," Rettenmund continued, "which is a plus because then you're almost a regular player. Then you maintain your timing on the off-speed pitches a little longer, but still, by the middle of the season, if you're a pinch hitter, you have no more timing on the off-speed pitches—you're not playing enough to time the ball. So if they throw a fastball and you're a pinch hitter, you better hit that bugger."

He said that a pinch hitter's timing is so hard to maintain because it can't be done just by taking batting practice. Facing live pitching is vital.

He further observed, "All pinch hitters have two things in common: first, they can hit the velocity. Second, they don't have a lot of movement; they don't have a big swing, like a hitch. You can't have a hitch and a lot of crap going on with your swing because you've got to make sure you hit that ball when you get it."

Rettenmund said that some of the best at this craft are Manny Mota, Jose Morales, and Lenny Harris. "Terry Crowley was good, too. It's a great job, and the amazing thing is that the one year I had the 96 pinch-hit appearances, I had 35 walks. The nice part about that is I realized halfway through the year that I couldn't hit a breaking ball, so I just didn't swing. And I was fortunate enough no one threw enough of them over [for strikes]."

Rettenmund detailed what made Cliff Johnson such a special pinch hitter. "He was a big line-drive hitter, but he had a short, little swing. That man was a good hitter—great, great fastball hitter. He was 6′3″ or 4″ and 240 pounds, and he used about a 30-ounce bat, a little bat, but, boy, could he gear it up for a heater. And he could hit it to the middle of the field." That, in part, made it possible for him to hit well as a pinch hitter while also setting the mark for the most career pinch homers (20).

Pinch hitters sometimes borrowed a teammate's talent, so to speak. Lee Smith commented, "I didn't need a hitter [to stand in there] when I warmed up, but some of the guys wanted to see the ball, like the pinch hitters who would be in the bullpen. You could do that in Wrigley Field because the bullpen was right down there, about 100 feet from the dugout, and guys would come into the bullpen. Now I don't think you're allowed to have a bat in the bullpen because of brawls—I think one guy came out of the bullpen with a bat one time. But back then some of the guys wanted to get up there [to stand in] and see the ball through the zone. I didn't mind it at all."

In summary, secrets to hitting while coming off the bench include (1) being prepared at all times, (2) staying loose (often by taking cuts in an area, near the dugout, provided in new parks for hitting), (3) being able to get ready in a hurry, (4) anticipating when you will be used, and (5) hitting well with two strikes—often being able to "spoil," or foul off, pitchers' offerings that are too close to take since an umpire might feel they nipped the strike zone.

A beneficial method of hitting that's almost as old as the game itself is switch hitting, which experts feel should begin around the age of seven years, about the same time the young player first effectively works at becoming a hitter in general. Few star switch hitters first learned that skill when older than that.

Second baseman Carlos Baerga felt Rose looked pretty much the same at the plate batting lefty and righty. As for himself, he stated, "I kinda' look a little bit different, and I use a lighter bat from the right side. I know

Robbie Alomar [does] the same thing." Baerga's logic for using different bats was simple. "My swing's a little bit quicker from the left side than the right side. Sometimes I wonder, 'Why is that [so]?' Maybe it's the reaction that you have to the ball, and when you face more pitchers from one side it's going to be that way." So he used a 34/32 from the left side and a 34/31 from the right side.

He pointed out, "It takes a lot of work to be a switch hitter. You're going to face more righties than lefties so you have to work really hard to maintain both sides." Agreeing with Baerga, Roberto Alomar said, "I try to hit from both sides in BP [as much] as I can."

To stay sharp both ways gives switch hitters a decided edge in that the batter never has to go left-handed against a lefty or right-handed against a righty.

In 2001 Orioles coach Tom Trebelhorn said that budding star Tim Raines Jr. didn't take to switch hitting until high school. Raines was frustrated for a while, but gained confidence. At one point he was going to give up hitting from the left side altogether, but his father convinced him not to quit. Incidentally, Raines Sr. also required some time and lots of toil to master switch hitting.

"Ultimately," said Trebelhorn of Raines Jr., "the left side became stronger. You see more right-handed pitching; you hit left-handed more often. I think if you stick with it and have the athleticism, you've got a chance to have your off-side be your best side. That happens to quite a few hitters."

Still, some pros that have switch-hit actually abandon that tactic if they feel they're not at least close to being equally skilled from both sides of the plate. San Francisco's J. T. Snow, for one, did that after slumping for a long period of time from one side. He had been a switch hitter from childhood on up through the professional ranks. Then, after his tenth pro season, when his average plummeted to a meager .248 in 1998, he reverted to hitting lefty exclusively. The next two seasons he hit .274 and .284 while his RBI and home-run total also prospered. However, still a bit weak against lefties, he slowed down to .246 in both 2001 and 2002.

Occasionally a switch hitter facing a left-handed pitcher chooses to give up his advantage of batting righty; he actually turns around and goes at the southpaw while hitting lefty. This usually happens when a switch hitter has had a history of frustration against a given pitcher. For instance, in the third game of the 1999 Division Series between the Atlanta Braves and the Houston Astros, Carl Everett, an outfielder who had great numbers in the regular season (.325, 25 HR, 108 RBIs), faced lefty Tom Glavine, a Cy Young Award winner. Everett had a 1-for-12 lifetime record against the tough pitcher, so he figured, "What the heck, I'll try batting left-handed against him."

Everett, a veteran, was tailoring his hitting to his capabilities and to his limitations. It's a fact that it takes considerable time for a young hitter to get to know himself. For example, when it comes to being patient at the plate, Shea Hillenbrand of the Diamondbacks has been a study of contrasts. In his rookie season he walked only 13 times in 493 plate appearances while seeing a league-low 3.25 pitches each time he hit. He admitted he had no plan of attack. By way of contrast, a veteran hitter like Robbie Alomar has long known how vital it is to look over pitchers' offerings.

By early May of Hillenbrand's sophomore season he began to realize he needed to work on his patience and it paid off well. He drew his seventh walk of the year nearly three months earlier than he had just one year before. He developed his new style by watching videotape of every one of his at-bats from his initial season, lamenting, "Most of the time last year I got myself out." Opposing managers candidly revealed they had told their pitchers to go at him by not throwing strikes.

Hillenbrand told *Sports Illustrated* that by the spring of 2002 he focused on changing his style by looking for pitches in certain spots early in his at-bat, and laying off all other offerings. "Last year," he said, "I'd go into my third at-bat having seen only three or four pitches. Now I see that many in my first at-bat. I've already seen everything a pitcher has."

Similarly, coach Robby Thompson offered a stylistic tip to young hitters, which is simple, but perhaps that's what makes it a universal truth: "You gotta know the strike zone. Pitchers are not going to throw it right over the heart of the plate for you and make those mistakes. So, you've got to know what are strikes and what aren't." In the minors, pitchers aren't quite as sharp with their control; they miss more often on their location. Thus, more mistakes are served up to drooling hitters.

There's also a theory that if a batter was a thinking man he would try to learn to think like a pitcher, then take the basic precepts of the mound with him as he enters the batter's box. Terry Mulholland, a veteran southpaw, concurs. "I know as a pitcher if I know what's inside a hitter's head, that gives me an idea on where I don't want to throw the ball. Obviously, if a hitter were wanting to get ahead of the game, or at least have an inside track on what pitchers thought, he would definitely sit down and talk with [pitchers] on his team. If he's a right-handed hitter, he may get an idea on how a right-handed pitcher likes to start guys off, or just get one of his teammate's impressions on what kind of hitter he is and how he would go about pitching him."

Mulholland says he's seen players do this, and the results really are informative and beneficial. Teammates generally will share such information and do almost anything along these lines to help each other out. That would seem like a sticky issue in the age of free agency because somewhere down the road the helpful pitcher may have to face the very hitter that he once advised.

He disclosed that generally a pitcher would only go so far in sharing information. Well aware that he may have to get this teammate out someday in the future, the pitcher will, says Mulholland, hold some information back because one simply doesn't "give away all his trade secrets." He says he refuses to go that far. Like a child with a cherished toy, sharing is nice, but only up to a point.

Sometimes a hitter will alter his basic style. For example, when the defense employs an infield shift, some hitters will purposely go the other way to defeat it or lay down a bunt to, say, third base if the defender is playing deep.

On August 15, 2000, Oakland put an infield shift on powerful Jim Thome. A's manager Art Howe packed three infielders between first and second base with their third baseman, Eric Chavez, playing where the shortstop normally would. This prompted Thome to comment, "It's frustrating, but I guess it's a sign of respect, too." According to a *Cleveland Plain Dealer* article, at that point in the season Thome had lost about 20 hits due to shifts.

That led Thome, who says the shifting against him began in 1999, to say, "It's one thing to face the shift when you're hitting .240 like I was earlier in the year. Now I've got my average back close to .290. That's when you start thinking about those 20 hits [about 50 points off his average] you lost."

Earlier that season, during Cleveland's home opener, Thome was at the plate in the first inning with two outs and nobody on base. The Texas third baseman, Tom Evans, was playing Thome to pull so drastically, he was almost at second base. Thome laid down a bunt. "It was my decision," admitted Thome. "It was strictly instinct."

It was his first bunt in 3,110 big-league at-bats. He had only one major-league sacrifice bunt ever, in the 1997 Division Series against the Yankees.

His inclination to lay one down was a highly questionable move; even Texas pitcher Rick Helling said, "I was a bit surprised. But if he wants to bunt four times in a row against me, he's more than welcome to keep bunting. I'd rather have him do that than hit one 480 feet." Even if Thome had beat out the bunt, a two-out single is usually harmless.

Cleveland manager Charlie Manuel diplomatically revealed, "I didn't mind him trying to bunt except that there were two outs, and with two outs and the wind blowing out to right field I'd like to see him swing away. He just has to handle the bat a little and concentrate on the situation."

In this age of prolific power, managers prefer their strong hitters remain loyal to the long ball, even when trying to thwart a shift. Long-time manager Buck Showalter philosophized, "I think with the home run being such a prevalent thing in today's game, more guys are more likely to stay with an approach to hitting regardless of what you do defensively." Thus, pull hitters earning astronomical salaries often won't change their ways.

He continued, "They're not going to try to say, 'OK, you're playing over there, I'm going to try to hit it over *there*.' They're going to say, 'Last time I looked, you can't put outfielders in the stands, so I'm going to try to hit the ball where grass doesn't grow.' You can't defend a home run. It's like trying to defend a foul ball—there's no reason to try to do it."

Of course, hitters can take a totally different approach and simply cheat. Batters have been known to cheat when they're in the box by sneaking a peek back at the catcher prior to the pitcher releasing the ball. If, the batter reasons, he can spot the location where the catcher is setting up, he'll have an idea where and perhaps how the pitcher is going to work him. Catcher Michael Barrett acknowledged, "I think some hitters do this [against us]. You have to be careful when you're catching that guys may do that."

Although it would seem logical that a catcher who is aware of this trick could simply let the batter take his peek, then cross him up, Barrett, a four-year veteran through 2003, said that it's not all that simple. Sometimes he is able to mess with their minds and fool them, but "the ones that do it the best, I probably still don't even know that they do it. But a lot of hitters now, especially with the Oakleys [dark sunglasses], will take a peek just to see where you're setting up more than anything and it can be tough to detect."

Although some hitters do employ this secret advantage of hitting, Barrett warned, "There's still no guarantee [the batter will know where the ball is headed]. The percentage of knowing where the ball is really going to be is tough—I mean, they really have to know the pitcher and know that he's going to hit his spot. A lot of times guys are effectively wild and won't even come close to hitting the target."

Hitters try for any advantage they can manage. If a pitcher gives away his upcoming pitch by any tell-tale sign, however slight, hitters will definitely pick up on it. In *The Babe Ruth Story* such a situation was depicted, albeit exaggerated. William Bendix, playing the title role, developed the habit of sticking his tongue out just before throwing his curve.

The pennant-winning Giants of 1951 under Leo Durocher reportedly used the rather shady tactic of stealing catchers' signals from a location inside the scoreboard.

While not all hitters like to know what pitch is forthcoming, those who *do* enjoy being forewarned say it helps them a great deal.

Another tactic is the use of illegal bats (see Chapter 10 for more), which some players believe helps the ball travel farther. If nothing else, a corked bat is lighter and allows hitters to get around on balls quicker. There is also the psychological factor: if a player believes a corked bat helps, then to him it does. Interestingly, Ruth wanted to use the heaviest bat he could swing; no corking for him.

One final obscure point of hitters' styles goes back to the days of Durocher. He supposedly instructed a young Willie Mays to wear his uniform pants high, showing a lot of his socks. This gave umpires the illusion of a smaller strike zone.

In short, it seems obvious that there are many schools of thought when it comes to hitting. Some batters' styles and theories of hitting are as complex (and develop as slowly) as a soap opera story line, while others are simple. Some methods produce power, some are conducive to contact hitting, and some (in the proper hands) result in hitting for both power and contact. The main concern for a hitter is that he should have a plan that fits his style, one that he can execute faithfully and successfully.

2

Hitters' Techniques and Strategies

FROM TY COBB's unusual grip to Stan Musial's peek-a-boo batting stance to Tony Batista's open-faced stance and Ichiro Suzuki's multipronged approach to batting, hitters have employed many unusual and interesting techniques and strategies for success.

And they'd better develop them very well. The average major-league fastball gets to the plate in less than a half a second, about .4 of a second to be more precise. That gives the hitter about one-fifth of a second to commit himself to a swing.

Hitting a round ball with a round bat and doing so squarely is a difficult task at any level of baseball. The phrase may be a cliché, but became one because it is universally true. To hit successfully at the major-league level is a seemingly impossible skill. Other players over the years have joked, too, about how a .300 hitter is still a failure 70 percent of the time. Since the total time that a bat meets the ball is a mere one hundredth of a second, it's no wonder great hitters are so rare. The odds of any player even making it to the major leagues are about 250,000-to-1.

Therefore, once again, players' techniques and strategies to improve their rate of success are of paramount importance. Musial used the same hitting approach for decades. The all-time great from Donora, Pennsylvania, said he always looked for a fastball, and then if he recognized he was getting something other than the heater, he would adjust to it. He felt he could delay his swing for a slower pitch but could not do the opposite on a faster offering. If he was guessing breaking ball and got a fastball, he wouldn't be able to catch up with it.

Further, while it was hardly an insight that only Musial possessed, he knew that it was vital to study pitchers so he knew not only their repertoire but also how their ball moved on their various pitches.

Musial once said, only half jokingly, "The secret of hitting is physical relaxation, mental concentration—and don't hit the fly ball to center."

Some hitters' techniques and training began in early childhood. All-Star Gregg Jefferies gained a great deal of attention when countless publications told of his unique training methods, his tools, and his talent. However, not all the tales they told were accurate.

Stories about a youthful Jefferies swinging a bat as many as one hundred times left-handed then one hundred times right-handed while standing in a swimming pool, with the water offering resistance to his swings were, he says, "really exaggerated. I probably did that once or twice, and *Sports Illustrated* wanted to make a big deal about it. I just ran with it, but I only did it a couple of times."

As far as training with his father, he did say his father "would 'x' tennis balls and he'd throw breaking balls so I'd see the 'x' move."

Scott Spiezio, a key member of the 2002 champion Angels, said that he was grateful that his training began early. He said that he and his father Ed, a former big leaguer, began a really serious routine when Scott was around three years old. They would work out every day with Scott using a Julian Javier give-away bat. Ed drilled holes in it so his tiny son could handle it. Scott recalled, "It looked like a woodpecker got hold of it." Still, as a step up from using a wiffle bat, it worked for him.

They were big on hitting tennis balls and early efforts at switch hitting. Scott succeeded from the outset. He stated, "When I started getting old enough to hit the neighbors' houses, we moved to the backyard. We had two pitching mounds in the backyard." Ed would throw BP to his son tirelessly.

In the unforgiving Chicago winter, they'd train in their basement with Scott hitting a ball suspended by a string while standing on a balance beam. He'd also hit a carpet-like padding wrapped around a pole to develop power. Scott often hit off a tee, driving ball after ball into a blanket. Emulating old-timers, he'd stand in front of a mirror and take cuts, checking to see if he looked mechanically sound.

Ed liked him to begin practices by dropping about 150 bunts, causing Scott to follow the ball from the pitcher's hand to his bat. Further, as the BP pitcher, Ed would work his son the way a big-league pitcher might—working high and tight, then going low and away before throwing low and inside.

David Segui's father, former big-league pitcher Diego, also taught his son inside baseball information when David was growing up, by pointing out situations on television, stressing how pitchers think and how they attack hitters.

David commented, "It makes you realize from an early age that the guy's not standing on the mound just throwing the ball over the plate." He said many fans rip a pitcher who has just thrown way out of the zone on a hitter, puzzled at how a pro could miss his target so badly. "Well," explained Segui, "he's setting something up. So you realize that there's actually another whole side of the game you don't see going on."

Players know that certain parts of their body are essential for good hitting technique. Williams stressed how important wrists are. He frequently spoke about what some younger players might not realize: in his cut, Williams's wrists rolled after the ball has left his bat, rolling not unlike the way a prize-fighter's fist drives into an opponent's face.

Former catcher Lance Parrish shared, "It doesn't necessarily take a big man to hit a ball a long ways. I remember seeing [Lou] Whitaker [5′ 11″, 180 pounds] hit one over the roof at Tiger Stadium. It's wrists, it's bat speed, it's everything put together."

Manager Sparky Anderson, who won World Series titles in both Cincinnati and Detroit, said he liked players such as Ernie Banks and Aaron because they had fast hands. He said that many sluggers have been big guys, but Banks and Aaron were exceptions. Hitters such as Aaron made it a point to work on their hand/bat speed while they were in the batting cage. And, of course, Aaron was known for his great wrists as well.

One of Brett's finest attributes was his ability to use his hands. An aggressive hitter and student of hitting, Brett was seldom fooled by a pitch. Thus, he made contact and avoided strikeouts. Jim Frey, who managed the three-time batting champ in Kansas City, once exaggerated that Brett "could get good wood on an aspirin."

According to another Tigers great, Alan Trammell, "There are different ways of hitting. There are guys who 'back-leg,' where you drop your back leg and you drive; your weight is more distributed middle to back. Walt Hriniak or Charlie Lau's theory was to get the weight back to start and then go forward; you get more of a weight transfer. Certainly you can't do that too fast; hitting's all timing whether or not you start on your back side a little bit longer or you go forward.

"When you drop and drive off your back leg, you're looking at guys who predominantly hit for a little bit more power—maybe strike out a little bit more. The guys that Charlie Lau or Walt Hriniak [worked with] went a little more forward after they started back. Those guys [would have higher averages]. Their bats stayed in the hitting zone a little bit longer and they were looking to hit the ball to all fields and to hit more line drives."

Brett, Lau's strongest evidence for the efficacy of his theories, comes to mind most often when discussing this latter type of hitter. When Hriniak's name comes up, most experts think of his best pupil, Wade Boggs.

Trammell added, "Walt was kind of a disciple of Lau's theory, but he took a couple of things and changed them. Basically they were kind of the same philosophies, but with some small things changed."

Willie Upshaw, a solid hitter during his ten-year career, feels that many young players, such as those just out of high school, must master certain concepts and skills if they are to make it as professional hitters. They have to "learn how to get behind the ball and stay closed. From there it's learning how to use your hands. Don't open up too soon, don't push the ball—throw the bat at the ball and hit the ball consistently where it's pitched." After all that, it's just a matter of a young hitter "catching up to the speed of the game" since there is no doubt that the game played at the big-league level is vastly different than what he has experienced before. "That's tough for young hitters," he emphasized.

Buck Showalter said that rookie hitters are quickly tested to see what they can and can't cope with. "Young hitters are going to get tested with a fastball, especially early on their arrival. And, after that, if they show they can handle that, then people are going to throw the kitchen sink at them."

Hitters, no matter how talented, are aware that they can't get by merely relying on their physical skills. They are wise, for example, to study opposing pitchers—their individual styles, habits, and abilities. If a given hurler is the type who is always around the plate with his pitches, trying to get ahead of hitters, then a batter should think basic strategies such as "Look for a first-pitch fastball." That's a philosophy that goes back to Little League, where, at one time, pitchers were permitted to throw nothing but fastballs. Even in high school most pitchers simply don't own very good curves, so hitters for eons have sat on fastballs. For that matter, big-league pitchers concede that the fastball is the easiest one to throw for strikes, so they throw them often. Everything revolves around the fastball.

Another example of knowing the opposing pitcher: if a pitcher likes to work fast, some hitters will simply step out of the box on him, a logical, but not always employed tactic. The desired effect is to control the pace, to get more time to concentrate, perhaps to agitate and to upset the pitcher.

Further, if a pitcher is struggling, hitters should display more patience at the plate, not chasing pitches that may be on the border or out of the zone. In other words, they should try to make the pitcher work a bit harder. Often a pitcher may even begin to aim the ball and become wilder, or, better yet, he may groove a fat pitch.

Not only that, if a starting pitcher can be induced to give up, say, a leadoff walk in an inning, he will be forced to work out of the stretch, a spot most starters find to be less comfortable than working out of the windup. Plus, their fastballs lose some velocity when they pitch from the stretch.

Brian Graham, a Cleveland coach in 1999, said this about specific techniques of hitting against various pitchers: "The game situation dictates your approach offensively. With some pitchers, even if Pedro Martinez is late into a game, you want to get a pitch you can hit. Because if he gets ahead of you, he has such an array of pitches that you're in trouble.

"So, you better get a pitch to hit, and if it happens to be the first pitch, you better take your shot at the first pitch. He's got a lot better chance of nibbling once he gets ahead of you in that situation.

"If it's Roberto Hernandez, you take a strike because you never know if he's going to be right around the plate all the time. You definitely take a strike on Jose Mesa because his out pitch is the fastball and his get-ahead pitch is the fastball. He's got to get it over the plate, so you're still going to get a chance at the fastball later in the count.

"It depends on who the pitcher is and who's hitting behind you, too. If you're down at the end of the order and you have a guy who's not going to hit a home run, then it's a tough call," he concluded.

Hitters even take cuts before they face the pitcher. Typically, in youth baseball, the leadoff hitter of an inning stands as close to the batter's box as he can, taking a swing, a dry cut, at the pitcher's warm-up tosses.

In some states, umpires no longer allow players to do this, fearing injury. Still, at the major-league level some hitters do make it a point to get close to the box as if clinging to their Little League habit. Upshaw said, "Cliff Johnson got so close to the box [instead of staying in the on-deck circle], the ump yelled at him," smiled Upshaw.

Matt Williams, recently retired third baseman, also had a scheme for preparing while in the on-deck circle. He said that he tried to time the fastest pitch when the pitcher was warming up or when that pitcher was working the man who hit ahead of him. "With the Giants, I had an advantage in hitting behind Kevin Mitchell because we are both pull hitters. Basically, they pitch us both the same way. If the pitcher would start Kevin off with a fastball high and inside, usually it would be the same pattern with me."

In the meantime, it took Kansas City's Mike Sweeney some time to become a solid hitter, but by 1999 he showed power. However, even then he said to succeed he had to "relax, try to stay through the middle of the field and hit balls gap to gap." He said batting woes happen when his swing becomes "too big and I try to pull balls. I need to keep my swing short."

Some say a hitter will never become a superstar if he can't hit with two strikes. Wagner noted, "Wade Boggs and Tony Gwynn were two of the best [two-strike hitters] I've seen because they're not going to try to jerk you out of the park, they're trying to put the bat on the ball. It makes it tougher [on the pitcher] when you get two strikes [on them]. I think they just have a great idea of the strike zone, and they know what they're capable of. And, they don't go out there and put any added pressure on themselves to hit a home run. They go out there and say, 'OK, I'm going to make contact.'"

Big Lee Smith, who faced more than his share of difficult outs, mused, "Don Mattingly and Keith Hernandez were tough guys because they would foul off really good pitches until the pitcher made a mistake or you made a pitch that they could hit. I used to throw Hernandez nasty forkballs on the black, and he'd flick that bat out there and foul them off. Then I'd throw a slider that wouldn't be that sharp, and 'Whack,' double down the line. I don't think I ever faced him when I didn't throw him six or seven pitches. I respected him, but I wanted to see him the next day because I knew that one day I would get him." With a self-deprecating chuckle, Smith added, "I'm going to wear him down, I guess."

"As for guys that I played *with*, Pedro Guerrero was at the top of my list [for hitting] with two strikes. He could flat-out hit with two strikes." Of active players Smith went with Barry Bonds, calling him "the best *any-strike* hitter, and it seems like the older he gets, the better he gets." For sheer ability with two strikes, Smith also likes "A-Rod, and I've got a lot of respect for Manny Ramirez, and I think [Gary] Sheffield's a great one, and the kid [Shawn] Green in L.A. is a good one.

"There's not a whole lot of guys who strike out a lot like Rob Deer and all those guys when I was coming through. Very few guys—Richie Sexson, a couple of kids like that."

Thome is unusual in that he fans often, yet he has a good eye. Baerga felt that gave Thome an edge, since he hits for power and "has a lot of walks, too. You can't just go over there and try to swing at everything they throw you. You have to have good discipline at the plate. Thome was more patient than [Albert] Belle [and many other sluggers]."

Some coaches tell young hitters that a wise two-strike approach to hitting includes spreading the feet, taking on a different mental attitude, moving closer to the plate, and striving, at all costs, to make contact. Rettenmund, a man whose ideas are clearly not those rattled off by so many instructors, disagrees. For example, he opined, "If there's such a thing as a two-strike approach and it's really better than your first-pitch approach or your 3-0 approach, then you should use that all the time."

Unlike those who advocate choking up, Rettenmund insists, "When you start making adjustments not to strike out, a lot of times you give yourself that lesson—the last thing you hear yourself saying is, 'Don't strike out,' and, damn it, you do.

"That's like saying, 'Oh, don't swing at a bad breaking ball in the dirt.' You don't swing, and the guy throws a heater right down the middle—a fastball *right there*—and you don't swing because you heard yourself say, 'Don't swing.'

"If your swing is solid, why would you make adjustments on every other pitch? The pitcher's not making those adjustments. I mean, he's out there nice and relaxed, he takes the sign, his hands are down low—and the hitter is standing there with a bat over his head, as tight as can be.

"It's similar to hitting a tennis ball or shooting pool—you get into position and the [stroke] goes back nice and easy and then comes forward. And all the work is done before you start the action—your preparation. You know what the pitcher is going to throw, and you know what you want to hit. So, you wait until he throws that pitch."

He reiterated that "once you start adjusting to the pitcher, you might as well come back [to the bench] because you're going to anyway. Don't even bother to carry the bat up to the plate."

Part of being a good hitter, even when behind in the count, is the batter's ability to stay loose. Some of the more relaxed hitters have their own unique ways to stay calm. Everett told the media that he always bats with a toothpick in his mouth, à la U. L. Washington, simply because "it relaxes me."

Likewise, most players don't hold their bat in a death grip, but hold it rather loosely. However, Ruth said he did grip the bat hard. He believed that type of grip allowed him to "swing it through the ball," which would result in the ball traveling greater distances.

All-time great Honus Wagner, like Keeler and Cobb, used to hit with a most unusual grip, spreading his hands apart. Cobb, however, would occasionally bring his hands together as he began his swing, depending on what he was anticipating, what the game situation was, and what he was trying to achieve.

Cobb's grip allowed him to gain excellent bat control, but gave him very little home-run power. The key was that his technique worked for him, especially during his era—the dead-ball time period. However, such a grip nowadays would probably belong to a weak hitter who might not last long in the majors (if he made it that far at all) in this era of power hitters. Even shortstops and second basemen today are expected to carry some punch on many teams.

Of course, almost all hitters agree that the bat should be held with the control coming from the fingers, rather than with the bat being set back deep in the palm of the hand. Great bat control leads to the ability to avoid strikeouts, often by fouling off, and thus spoiling, good pitches. Ichiro Suzuki, as pesky as a hangnail, said that, like Cap Anson, he too can intentionally foul off borderline pitches, forcing the pitcher to work hard and hopefully, ultimately, offer up a mistake pitch.

As for the actual swing, sometimes a player can work on a new approach to hitting that suddenly pays huge and immediate dividends. Such hitters are able to take their hitting ability up a notch, from being a good hitter to becoming a great one. While Upshaw believes that "most guys who can hit have always been able to hit," he mentioned men such as Brady Anderson who suddenly elevated their game.

Some hit for average and then added power to their package, while others hit for power while sacrificing their average, but later worked on that phase to become a complete hitter. Upshaw cited Shawn Green: "He could always hit [for average] but came into his power hitting lately. And Carlos Delgado—[he] hit for power and came into [hitting for] average.

"I had Palmeiro two years in Texas. He wanted to develop power, and he went about it the right way. Talk about a guy who became a total hitter. He learned the pitchers and the league, and his swing developed. Rafael sacrificed some average for power, but it all came together. He worked on being aggressive and learned to get in front of more balls."

Philadelphia's Mike Schmidt wrote in his book *The Mike Schmidt Study* that the best time to start the stride and begin the swing is usually just "when the ball passes the pitcher's head in his delivery, an instant *before* release." Schmidt also quoted Frank Robinson who asserted, "There is an area, a square somewhere next to each pitcher's head, where he'll release the ball, and I will follow his hand up into that square and see the ball come out of that square."

Individual techniques have always been a baffling issue. Cobb hit .367 lifetime while Williams checked in at .344. Yet their approaches were vastly different. Once they got into a lengthy discussion of hitting and wound up shouting at each other. If nothing else, this indicates that hitters can succeed using diverse methods.

This certainly makes sense. After all, a player should work his strengths. If a hitter has speed along the lines of a Brett Butler or a Carew, he should learn to hit down on the ball and work on his bunts. Such hits, over the course of a season, translate into an inflated batting average.

Carew had definite thoughts on his hitting technique. Instead of focusing on the strike zone and gearing his switch to the location of the pitch, as Williams did, Carew felt it was more important to be aware of what pitches he could handle and where to place those pitches for hits. Thus, instead of thinking about the rule-book strike zone, Carew worried about *his* own strike, or hitting, zone. He was willing to take a pitch for a strike quite often if he felt he wasn't ready to attack that pitch. So, staying within oneself was a cardinal rule to Carew—as was aggressively hitting the ball where it's pitched.

Carew's ideal grip was a loose one; he held the bat where the palm ends and the fingers begin, with the knuckles of the first joint of his hands lined up with each other. He also believed a short stride of no more than half a foot was perfect for him. His back foot was always deep in the box, on the chalk line—almost *out* of the box.

Experts realize that it's not where the bat starts prior to the hitter's cut, it's what position the bat is in as it comes forward. Good hitters have the bat in a ready, cocked position as their front foot touches the ground, starting their actual swing. That is also the moment when it's essential to pick up the ball out of the pitcher's release point—something they say Barry Bonds does as well or better than anyone in the game.

One odd style of hitting involves hitting with a hitch, like Joe Morgan did with his trademark flapping of an arm prior to a pitch. That's something no coach would teach his hitters. Hitting coach Tom McCraw explained that Morgan's hitch and similar ones didn't hurt hitters as long as "they keep their hands back." What appeared to be a flaw in Morgan's swing, or appeared to be a problem with Roberto Clemente hitting off his front foot, was as immaterial, as meaningless, as a mirage; if they kept their hands back, nothing else mattered.

Tigers manager Alan Trammell said players like Clemente got away with their unusual batting habits due to "great hand-eye coordination. That's God-given talent and [such players] certainly work very hard at it, but I'd say the good Lord gave them a little extra.

"There are certain guys who aren't the norm as far as their technique. But when you look at guys, for example, Carl Yastrzemski, with the hands held high—well, actually, he didn't hit from there. That was just a trigger, a starting point.

"A lot of things happen, even with Roberto Clemente and his front foot stepping out. He still had his 'behind' behind him where he had something that he could at least 'throw.' So, if you really looked at it on film, you could break some things down and say there are a lot of similarities. Even though there might be small technique differences [among such hitters], [there are] a lot of similarities in the overall swing."

Many times when Clemente's swing looked awkward, almost as if he was bailing out, he'd flick at the ball and hit it to the opposite field. One could say that he was a bad-ball hitter at times, but if he liked a bad ball and could hit it well, why not do that? Trammell concurred, "I'd have to say, yes, if he could hit it, then it was something that he could handle. And, again, there are always exceptions to the rule, and he would be one of them."

Trammell mentioned another hitter with an unusual style: "Julio Franco. [He] holds the bat high, wraps the bat—and that's not normal." He stressed a coach certainly would not teach such an approach to hitting, but it feels comfortable for Franco.

"Gary Sheffield waggles his bat; the bat head goes forward. But if you would look at that on film, he's got such great hand-eye coordination and his wrists are so strong that when the ball is crossing into the hitter's zone, his bat is back and it's not so much forward as you would assume [when looking at it live]—it's like it's an illusion. Again, if you were to break his swing down frame by frame, you would see that it's pretty good. And, of course, we know what kind of bat speed he generates."

Again, whether a hitter has a traditional approach to the game or whether he stands there like a Willie Stargell turning his bat into a windmill prior to a pitch, batters can have success using diverse methods. After all, Musial succeeded even though some said that when he stood at the plate he looked like a mischievous little boy peering around the corner to see if the coast was clear. Yet somehow he managed to lash out 3,630 lifetime hits with relative ease.

Ichiro is another interesting case. In his first spring training in the United States, he didn't overly impress Mariners manager Lou Piniella with his hitting technique, continually slapping at the ball. When Piniella asked him to try to pull the ball, Ichiro informed his boss that while he certainly could pull, he was setting the pitchers up by not showing them that ability.

Sure enough, once the regular season began, according to teammate Al Martin, "He became a completely different player. . . . You saw him drive the ball. You saw him slap the ball. You saw him do what the hell he wanted with the ball." Fellow Mariners found out that Ichiro had at least five different bat techniques, including one in which he runs up on the ball, gains about a two- or three-step head start toward first base, and hits it with one hand. Using another technique, he basically leans into the pitch and pokes at it. Occasionally he even takes a power cut.

Carlos Baerga put up some great stats during his days with Cleveland. In fact, he did something that only one other second baseman ever did. He hit over .300 with 200 hits, 20+ homers and doubles, and over 100 runs and RBIs. The other second sacker to do this was the immortal Rogers Hornsby.

Later, Baerga experienced the nadir of his career when he bounced around from team to team, including stints in the minors and even in Korea. By 2002 he rebounded and was back in the majors with Boston, hitting .286. Besides the obvious tip of never giving up, he also itemized several other strategies he followed for success.

He began, "There's nothing secret; it's just when you work, you deserve to have success. I watched a lot of the good hitters. I got the chance to come back and play with Tony Gwynn in '99, and I watched what he did every day. He was always in the cage, and he always maintained the swing and watched video.

"It's not just 'Come to the ballpark and show up to the field and hit.' It takes a lot of work to maintain your swing, especially when you're a switch hitter. You have to hit the same from both sides, not just one, and keep a nice balanced swing, good balance in your body, always watching the ball as the pitcher lets it go from his arm, and use the whole field.

"When you use the whole field, you're going to be a .300 hitter. If you just try to pull the ball and just try to hit home runs, you might hit for power, but you're never going to hit for average. And, if you want to bring a lot of RBIs, you have to use the whole field. So, that's the key to me to becoming a good hitter."

Baerga reflected on the years when he was hitting for average and power. "That's the key," he reiterated, "when you use the whole field, I would say that you can put up some good numbers; and if you don't strike out too much, you can put good numbers. I always say if you make contact, you're going to find a hole, but if you strike out a lot, it's going to be hard. Maybe Sammy Sosa [can] strike out a lot but can put up a lot of RBIs and keeps putting up good numbers, but when you don't strike out a lot, you have a chance to [pick up] an RBI somewhere."

He also spoke of *how* and *where* he wants to hit the ball. He shoots for line drives, realizing that "if you try to hit a lot of fly balls, now you've got so many good outfielders, they're going to catch it. So if you try to hit line drives, if you hit it hard, the ball's going to go no matter what."

Ideally, as Baerga touched upon, hitters should have the ability to hit to all fields, yet it's well known that some sluggers can't (or won't) do that. Terry Francona, who began his coaching career as a hitting instructor in 1991, commented on the dichotomy of hitting strategies: "A guy like Ichiro can lead the league in hitting because he *does* use all the field. He's going to get more than his share of soft hits because you can't defense the whole field. He deserves those hits.

"Some power hitters—guys like [Mark] McGwire—they don't *need* to [use the whole field]; they're trying to hit the ball out of the ballpark. They don't want to get 20 points on their batting average and lose 20 RBIs; they're trying to get production. So it just depends on who you are. But if you use more field, you're going to get more hits."

Galarraga has his own philosophy concerning hitting. "The main thing," he said, "is a lot of work and [the fact that] I played baseball all my life—that's what I like to do— and a lot of hitting, a lot of practice. Plus God helped me to help my dream come true to be a professional hitter." So, he feels that it takes both a natural talent and a lot of diligent work.

"In addition to that, we've got a lot of people in baseball to help. You have to see the ball and you have to see it with both eyes. You have to follow through and you have to stay back [on the ball]. It's a little bit of mechanics, too."

Yet another beneficial technique is that of working the count. Rettenmund said, "For whatever reason, I took a lot of pitches and a lot of base on balls in my career. I don't know why; no one told me to do it that way. And I know that everyone right now in baseball is trying to teach working the count. How do you work a count? I didn't even know I was working a count, but I think I had [something] like 600 base on balls and 400 strikeouts [he had 445 and 382 exactly].

"My on-base percentages were always high, but nowadays the game has changed a lot. You've got guys in baseball now who talk [about a theory] because it sounds good, but do you want to see a Frank Thomas have a .430 on-base percentage? Once you get him on, you can't get him around. It's a waste."

Aware of the comparison between Thomas and Williams, who was also highly selective, drawing an abundance of walks, Rettenmund said that Williams "might have been able to out-run Thomas. Frank—you can't get him from first to home; it takes three hits."

So, Rettenmund believes there certainly are "guys you want up there working the count, and there are guys who are really good at it—those guys are very valuable." However, someone like Thomas isn't such a player.

Rettenmund further stated, "I think the only way you can work the count, and it's my opinion, is you have one pitch and you have an area [you're looking for], and if he throws there on the first pitch, whack it. If it's not there, take it. And, after that, you've got to go battling and wait for it; and if you're ahead in the count, you can wait longer, but had better not miss anything he throws in your area—and you know where your area is before you go up there. That's how I think you work a pitcher."

Roberto Alomar is also skilled at making the pitcher toil while looking over a basketful of pitches until he's able to pick out one that's to his liking. In 1999, for example, he saw more pitches than almost any other hitter in baseball (2,946). He said, "I've always been a patient hitter. I like to make the pitcher work. I don't like to give him any easy outs. If I can make him throw me four, five, or six pitches and the other guys can do the same, that pitcher is going to be tired by the sixth or seventh inning."

It's pretty fundamental: make the pitcher throw numerous pitches — which in turn allows the hitter to see a slew of them. Patient hitters such as Alomar, who force a lot of pitches, don't lunge after first pitches as some hitters do. Alomar's theory is that the more pitches you force the pitcher to throw, the more likely he will make a mistake and you will get a really good pitch to drive.

Between 1992 and 2000, the average number of pitches per plate appearance for major leaguers went up from 3.69 to 3.8, meaning the average hitter was learning to be a bit more patient, as if following the lead of hitters such as Alomar.

However, he also said, "If a pitcher is throwing strikes, it's a different story." In 1999, on occasions when Alomar felt pitchers were putting the ball over the plate, and he made contact with the first pitch, he hit a lusty .583 (21 for 36).

In short, a list of the elements that make up perfect hitting technique includes the following qualities and abilities: The body is relaxed. The swing is smooth, based on natural arm action and, generally, graceful motion. The feet are comfortable. The eyes, shoulders, and hips are level, with a solid, even distribution of weight. The bat starts back, triggered and ready to go. The ball is met, ideally, about a foot in front of the hitter's body with an emphatic shift of weight. The follow-through is clean and natural. The batter's head never jerks from the ball, having followed the ball from the pitcher's release point through contact.

3

Preparations and Routines

GAME-DAY PREPARATION begins from the moment a player wakes up and thinks about that day's contest. When he walks into his clubhouse, he might glance at the bulletin board. There, long before game time, is a chart with the lineups for the game. A hitter can look at that posting and see who the opposing pitcher is that day as well as check on other facts about the hurler. The chart lists what pitches he throws and the typical speed of those pitches. It also includes the scouts' evaluations of that pitcher's control.

Another aspect of hitters' preparation that isn't physical is talking hitting. Players absolutely love to talk baseball. Perhaps no man delighted in such discussions more than Ted Williams did. Who can forget the scene at Fenway Park during the All-Star game just a few years ago when he was golf-carted onto the field? He was immediately engulfed by the throng of All-Stars who had already congregated on the diamond. Nobody minded that the start of the game was delayed as Williams, the hitting legend, held court, discussing his favorite topic, the most difficult thing to do in baseball: putting good wood on a ball.

Ted's favorite pupil was probably Tony Gwynn, but Professor Williams generously shared his insights with virtually any hitter he ever encountered. He was famous for strolling up to a young hitter at a batting cage during spring training and greeting him. After a few brief amenities, Williams would grill the youngster with questions such as, "What kind of pitch did you hit yesterday for that single to right?" and "What was the count when you flew out in the sixth inning?" Often the fledgling hitter was baffled. "I don't know. I just got a pitch I liked and hacked at it." Sorry, wrong answer for Williams.

When Ted met a fellow hitting enthusiast like Gwynn, though, their discussions took on Socratic substance and style. In fact, Gwynn sought out Williams many times, flying in to see him for an informal baseball seminar any chance he could grab.

As important as it is to talk baseball with teammates, it can be even more important to listen. As Boston great Wade Boggs said, when he was a rookie he was expected to shut up and listen. He felt that by being silent and respectful to veterans, he could absorb a great deal from those who had already been there.

It does benefit young players to listen and learn. Atlanta Assistant General Manager Frank Wren told USA Today/Baseball Weekly, "Until players get past their first few years in the big leagues, they're just feeling their way around." Typically, he believed that a player will start to blossom around the age of 25 or 26. It takes a blend of baseball theory coupled with playing time and experience to allow a player to bloom.

Incredibly, superstar catcher Mike Piazza was selected as a courtesy pick by the Dodgers in the distant 62nd round of the 1988 free-agent draft. Los Angeles picked him only as a favor to Dodger fixture Tommy Lasorda, a distant relative of Piazza.

Piazza is a fine mistake hitter who has great power to the opposite field, using his excellent bat speed to his advantage time and time again. It's been written that Piazza, as a youth, virtually memorized Williams's book on hitting.

He couldn't have picked a better role model. Even a man like Phillies manager Larry Bowa, who has been around the game for a very long time, was awed by Williams. "I met him one time. . . . It was like meeting the Pope. You look at him and say, 'Wow.' "

An aspect of preparation that many fans don't see is the life of players inside the clubhouse. Gene Clines was the hitting coach of the Mariners when they featured hitters such as Ken Griffey Jr., Edgar Martinez, and Jay Buhner. More recently Clines was with the National League Champion San Francisco Giants of '02. Clearly, then, he knows his hitters, and, being in so many successful teams' clubhouses, he knows what goes on there.

For example, during the 1970s his Pirates won many division titles. Clines said, "We'd come to the park early and spend three to four hours playing [cards to relax]. Winning teams come in early. When you're winning, you can't wait to get to the clubhouse—it gives you a burst of energy.

"It's just like a hitter when he's hitting well: he never gets tired. It's always the guys who aren't hitting who say they're tired. The clubhouse is your home away from home. You spend more time there than in your apartment. It's your own private domain." Most hitters agree they need a sort of Fortress of Solitude and need to relax prior to performing on the field.

Some fans think that players just goof around prior to a game. Ken Griffey Jr. said of those charges, "We're baseball players [professionals]; we know how to get ready." He did add that you do need time to unwind before a game. He said, "Once you have your clothes on, it's easy to relax in the clubhouse."

"Everybody's different," began former big leaguer Scott Pose. "I think even if it's just 20 minutes just to get away from everything, just so you don't even have to think about baseball, you can just read the paper. And that in itself is a way of getting mentally ready. I think it's tailor-made for every individual player.

"I just try to get by myself, think about what's going on during the game—who I'm going to face and how they might work me. It's as simple as that."

So, where does a player go to find asylum amidst a locker often populated by a mob of media, a pack of clubhouse attendants, and a herd of fellow players? Pose said some players could hide out in the trainer's room or other such areas that are off-limits to the media. However, when I talked with him, he said modestly, "Nobody's really clamoring for me [for interviews], so it's pretty easy for me to get away, but, yeah, I've been in New York where guys had to go to the players lounge just to get some time to be by themselves."

"A lot of guys," said Pose, "whenever they can, do video. A lot of guys will just talk to other guys about the game or just come in here [to the clubhouse] and relax, watch TV, and see highlights of the night before. I've seen a lot of different approaches. More often than not, the pitchers usually stay by themselves, and everybody's kind of wary about talking to them. But regular players—we play so much that it really doesn't matter, it's not as big a ritual."

Shortly after being voted into the Hall of Fame, Eddie Murray shared his feelings about how players should come to the park every day with the idea that they have something new to learn. "It's amazing the things you see," he said. "This is a thinking man's game. It's the ultimate chess game with every pitch thrown. You have to be on your game. Learning before you play [in the majors] simplifies it a little bit."

Men such as the obsessive Rose and Cobb didn't have to be lectured about learning the game; they intently devoted nearly every minute of the day preparing either directly or indirectly for their next game. Rose, for instance, said virtually every waking thought that he had was about the game. He scoured every box score seeking information, every possible edge.

Hornsby was unique. Aside from going to the racetrack in his spare time, he did little else. He refused to pore through the sporting pages like Rose did because he was so protective of his eyes, so dedicated to hitting. He wouldn't even go to the movies, since he felt that using his eyes in such a nonproductive way could only hurt them.

Another seldom-discussed preparation tip of major-league hitters is knowing the umpire working home plate. In youth leagues a player might see an umpire only a few times and not have the opportunity to study his strike zone. However, if that umpire is calling low strikes in the first inning, throughout the rest of that game a hitter should never take a low pitch when he has two strikes on him.

At the big-league level, all hitters know that certain umpires have wide strike zones (e.g., Eric Gregg, the ump whose generosity at the plate helped Livan Hernandez rack up a ton of strikeouts in a 1997 NLCS contest). Against them, a hitter should come to the plate hacking away. Other umpires, especially tall ones who don't like to bend as much as the smaller umps do, tend to call strikes a bit higher than most umpires do. All this must be factored into the thinking of a pro.

Jay Bell, a member of the 2001 World Series Champion Arizona Diamondbacks, spoke of other preparations a player does on game day. First of all, he said, one should be aware that "different players have different preparation. Certainly that's one of the things we try and figure out—which is appropriate for us throughout the course of the [days in the] minor leagues, how we have to prepare ourselves physically and mentally for the game. No two ways are alike."

However, Bell did say that he feels the mental preparation is, in many ways, more important than the physical. "For the most part, most of the guys here [in the majors] have a talent to play baseball that surpasses the average person. If they didn't have that talent, they wouldn't be at this level. So the athletic part of the playing side is already there. Now it's just a matter of making sure that you tap into that mental side of it and make sure that you learn which way to go about preparing yourself to allow you to have success during the game."

Bell is the type of player who gets to the park early to get his work in. "When I'm at home, I get to the park about two o'clock [about five hours before game time]; whenever I'm away [on the road], about two-thirty."

Bell said that watching game videos is a part of his game, part of the reason he's at the park so early. In the old days the concept of watching film was most associated with the sport of football. Now baseball is heavily into watching video. Bell said, "Each and every pitcher we face—we have video on and you try to pick up [his] tendencies and go from there."

Hitters who are videophiles say they benefit from zoning in on a given pitcher's release point. Others, including coaches, prefer to watch tape to see if a pitcher is tipping off his pitches. The ability to watch a delivery in slow motion or by using freeze frames is a huge advantage. Plus, many enjoy the benefits of simply getting a preview of the day's starting pitcher.

Cleveland infielder John McDonald's pregame approach involves many steps. "I just like to take flips in the cage, hit off the tee a little bit, do something to get my body loose, take regular BP and a little soft toss."

Buhner also talked about his routine. "I get here about one hour before the bus. Today, for example," he said when he was with Seattle, "I got here at ten-thirty [for a one-thirty game] and I got my treatment. Basically then I get my stuff ready for the game. I'll relax, play cards, and take BP. After BP, I remember what the starting pitcher threw me the last time I faced him. I watch videos; they really help. I can see the release point and the location on pitches. You can pick up tendencies."

Buhner elaborated, "Ninety percent of the game is mental; only ten percent is physical. Preparation is very important." He also pointed out that as the year winds down and players tire in the scorching August sun, "you have to step it up a bit—maybe for a salary drive and for your own personal pride [especially if your team is out of contention]. Some days when I'm not feeling as well as other days, it takes a little more time stretching and running [to prepare]."

He also has a postgame routine. "After the game," he continued, "I remove all the tape, ice my ankle down, and get a couple of carbohydrate drinks. Then I think about the day and file it away. Then it's back to the hotel."

Albert Belle not only came in early to get ready, he also stayed late, long after game's end. "When we're on the road, some of us come in for early defense or early hitting. Usually for a seven-thirty game I get there around five o'clock. I get there and get settled in. I get early stretching, hitting, and treatment. After a game I tend to stay and lift weights."

Conversely, when he was with the Mariners, Griffey Jr. said that after a contest he does two things: "I shower and go home. I take down my pants, jock strap, and socks all in one tug." The quick-change artist then relaxes until the next day.

Knowing the opposing pitcher is also vital. In youth leagues a hitter often studies the pitcher when he warms up before the game and between innings. It's not all that different in the majors. If a pitcher has a great fastball while warming up pregame, a hitter who studies him will be forewarned. Or, when a new pitcher gets called up to the majors, students of the game quickly memorize what the newcomer throws and what his go-to pitch is.

Preparation doesn't end in the clubhouse. Most of the big-name players on the 2002 Texas Rangers had interesting routines when they were on deck. Alex Rodriguez, Rafael Palmeiro, and Ivan Rodriguez all drifted away from the on-deck circle and stood near the circle chalked around home plate, so close that if they were high school players, the umpire would require them to back off. On nearly every pitch their eyes were trained on the pitcher and his delivery.

Leonard Koppett wrote that while in the on-deck circle, hitters should consider matters such as what the pitcher's best stuff is and "what is his best *today*? What sequence of pitches has he gotten me out with in the past? Knowing my weaknesses—which he does—how does he usually try to exploit them with his particular equipment?" Koppett also mentioned factoring in the game situation and the hitter's goal in that situation, as well as mulling over what pitch you *want* to hit. The thought process is complex, yet should become almost automatic, rote, for veteran hitters.

Other preparatory functions occur in the on-deck circle, such as applying pine tar to the bat. Further, hitters typically use a weight around their bat—either a long sleeve that fits around the bat, slipped over the knob until it fits snugly over the barrel of the bat, or a "doughnut."

Hitters always love to loosen up with such equipment. Long ago, they merely used two or more bats (muscular slugger Ted Kluszewski always seemed to have four bats in his hands as he took his warm-up cuts) to provide the weighted bat effect. Lead bats have been used, as have sledgehammers, a length of lead pipe, and even a strange device that looks like fins that fits over the bat. When a player takes a cut with such a device attached, the fins provide wind resistance, creating the same basic effect as using a lead bat.

As the hitter's turn to bat nears, with the current hitter going deeper into the count, men like A-Rod then like to take the weight off their bat and take some wicked cuts prior to stepping up to the plate.

Some players like to hit so much, they take their practice cuts in locales other than the on-deck circle. Players have been known to stand in front of mirrors, analyzing their cuts. Paul O'Neill would even take swings with an imaginary bat while he was playing the outfield.

It's not entirely clear if he was merely working on his muscle memory or whether he was thinking about hitting—perhaps what he had done in his last at-bat, and simply wanted to take some swings. However, sometimes between pitches to an enemy batter, O'Neill would actually move his arms in a bat-swinging motion—in effect, taking dry BP while in the field. When he was on the road, those actions would lead fans to get on him, but he didn't care—he was working on the part of the game he loved best.

Once in the box, there is still work to be done. Some fans claim that players waste time when they step out of the batter's box or that they're milking their television exposure. However, most of the time that hitter is either trying to settle down, regain his focus, or anticipate what pitch he will see next. All-Star third baseman Travis Fryman commented that the hitter is probably leafing through his memory bank for information on the pitcher that he's gained from video and "advance scouting reports that are pretty meticulous."

Fryman continued, "Most of the time you're thinking or calming yourself down a little bit, trying to back off a little bit, or just trying to relax a little bit in that situation. You might feel tense up there, or maybe you think a guy's going to throw a pitch here so you're hashing over some things. But very few guys are just stalling; there's a thought process behind it." Sometimes the batter is formulating an educated guess as to what to look for "based on what [he's] seen of that pitcher in the past."

Thome put it another way: "It's cat and mouse. You're trying to get any edge you can, and when you step out, you might be in a long at-bat and trying to get your composure back or your breath back and then just go from there."

Hornsby may not have spent time reading, but most hitters don't mind reading and writing when it comes to keeping a log on the pitchers they've faced. Some players literally keep a written record of each of their at-bats, while others keep a mental "book." That's not so easy now, though, with 30 big-league teams, with interleague play, and with so many mediocre pitchers coming and going in baseball's version of an Old West saloon's swinging door. Many hitters today keep their log on a computer. (See Chapter 5 for more on technology.)

Standout hitter Todd Helton is one of those many hitters who readies for his hitting chores by keeping a book (he calls it a "journal"). He said, "I started doing it my rookie year when I was struggling. I wrote down what pitchers threw me in different situations, and I sometimes refer back to it." He said that he recorded every single pitch, and that process in itself made him become introspective and analytical.

It's no wonder Billy Wagner said Helton is "one of the best hitters in baseball. He'll probably go on to be one of *the* best for power and average before his career is over."

In the meantime, Ted Williams felt that every single time he faced a pitcher it was an information-gathering opportunity, a chance to store more info into his mind. Imagine to what degree he would have taken his approach to the game if he had played in the era of modern technology.

In 2002 elder statesman Rickey Henderson said that he tells youngsters "about the love of this game and [how] they have to dedicate themselves to the game. Never give up on yourself. Work hard and you will accomplish things. I play the game because I love it. That's why I played it and why I'm playing it today—God gave me this talent." Such an approach is sure to help a player be prepared to play.

Many young players find that an excellent way to hone their skills and get a shot at the majors is by playing in a fall league. Anaheim's spunky David Eckstein said in the *Arizona Fall League 2002 Program* that that particular league helped him because the level of competition challenged him. "It gives you confidence to play with those guys and against those guys. I learned the game better and tested my skills against the best."

Because Eckstein is small by baseball standards (about 5′ 6″ or 7″ and 165 pounds), he had to work hard just to get a chance at making the majors. Granting that, he said, "You just try to do the things that will help you out. . . . At the plate I have to be patient and do whatever I can to get on base, including walks and getting hit by pitches. Whatever it takes—anything."

The scrappy Eckstein led the American League in both his rookie and second seasons in getting hit by pitches. He set a new record for getting plunked by a rookie (21) and followed it up with a painful 27 in 2002. "Yeah, it hurts," he said. "But my job is to get on base." Plus, unlike Barry Bonds, Eckstein boldly steps to the plate with no protective gear at all.

Friends have joked that his preparation for baseball includes allowing himself to get drilled by pitches in BP. That's not too far from what Ron Hunt, who holds the season record for being hit by a pitch with 50, did when he let himself get hit during old-timers games, "taking one for the team."

Actually, Eckstein, a fine leadoff hitter who chokes up on the bat, says one of the biggest ways he prepares is by staying mentally sharp. "At this level," he noted, "everyone has the physical tools, but it's the mental aspect that keeps you here." So, he is always aware of the count, works it well, and somehow continues to achieve even at the demanding big-league level.

The mental side of the game is also illustrated by all-time great Hank Greenberg, who once hit 58 home runs in a season (1938) and drove in 183 runs, the third-best total ever (1937). "Greenberg positively made a great hitter out of himself," said Baltimore Orioles executive Paul Richard. "He did it by constant practice. . . . He'd stay after games and hit until darkness made him quit."

Aaron's preparation included doing his homework. He said that in addition to keeping a mental book on pitchers, "When I'm hitting well, I can tell what a pitch will be when it's halfway to the plate. Guessing what the pitcher is throwing is about 80 percent of hitting. The other 20 percent is execution. All good hitters guess a lot; you're a dumb hitter if you don't guess some."

Part of Erstad's background—and ultimately his preparation for pro baseball—was playing another sport. The Angels' star outfielder declared, "I think playing football at Nebraska really helped. Playing in front of all those people and on national television in pressure situations—it was a really good learning experience for me."

Veteran Bill Haselman even spoke of how players' hands get ready for the season. A player's hands have to be strong and tough, and hitters often develop calluses as thick as two all-beef patties. Nowadays, players work all year round, but even if a player was coming off an injury and hadn't been in the cage for some time, Haselman pointed out, "Spring training alone is going to build [the hands] up. You hit enough in the cage and [off the] tee. You might go through some blisters in the beginning in January, but you're going to build [calluses] quick. I have never seen it be an issue for hitters as far as blisters where they can't swing a bat during the season."

So, he says, it's not so much an important matter of being sure the hands develop those calluses, it's simply that "they're going to get tough. You don't *try* to get them tough; if you swing a bat, they're going to get tough. It's like swinging an axe."

Journeyman Bill Selby basically agrees with Haselman, saying that since he hits in the off-season, especially since he has played a lot of winter ball, his hands are tough coming into the spring. In his case, then, callused hands are the norm, not the exception.

"I'd imagine if somebody didn't hit in the off-season, it would take a couple of weeks to get used to it because you're going to have to get over the sweat and blisters first." If a player is inactive, the hand toughness goes away. Selby said he avoids that. "I always play and I'm always doing something. If I'm lifting weights, it keeps the calluses on my hand. I try not to lose those calluses."

Haselman added another factor: batting gloves. "I think they definitely help. You've got a layer of leather between your hand and the bat, but if you looked at those guys' hands back in the [early years]—they swung the bat with no gloves—I think most of their hands would be tough as could be. Maybe not in spring training, but you know they're going to build it up." Sandpaper-rough hands, then, are the inevitable tools of the hitter's trade; they come with the job.

Players today tend to be better educated than those of long ago, yet still come across as being superstitious when it comes to having their rituals. "It's part of the game," said longtime vet Lee Stevens. "Every guy in here [the clubhouse] is superstitious, and they're lying if they say they're not because that's part of your routine and that's part of how you get mentally prepared to play this game. It's a crazy game, a real mental game, and everybody in here has a certain routine, whether it's your batting gloves, your clothes, what you eat for lunch, whatever. There are things on and off the field."

Stevens' argument may be a matter of semantics. For example, if a player always takes a shower at a certain time as part of his pregame routine, is that superstitious or is that merely his style, his way of doing things before a game?

"Your routine *is* a superstition," Stevens continued. "When you break that routine, you kind of get out of whack. Every player does that and tries to find one [routine] that he likes."

Then, if a player deviates from his routine and, for example, goes into a slump, he can explain his problems by attributing them to bad luck. It's a sort of self-fulfilling prophecy. "You think that [variation of routine] is why you didn't get any hits. So, you're superstitious and you don't even realize it sometimes. Whatever makes you feel better when you go out there to take the field [is fine]." Again, when players deviate from their groove, they often feel uneasy—not what hitters, notorious creatures of habit, want.

Like Williams, Boggs took his preparation for games very seriously. Boggs, in fact, epitomized the concept of having a set routine. His diet of eating almost nothing in the world other than various chicken dishes was well-chronicled, too.

Former infielder Jim Lefebvre said that Boggs certainly "has routines—he eats chicken at a certain time on game days, takes batting practice at an exact, specific time, [and] warms up and takes ground balls at a certain time."

Lefebvre says this kind of behavior is beneficial. "Boggs is probably one of the most prepared persons in the game. That's why he's so successful. It's not a superstition, it's just a form of preparation," he concluded, echoing the words of Stevens.

Cubs superstar Sammy Sosa is the type of player, and there are many like him, who arrives very early at the park. He, too, then follows a definite pattern, which includes stretching, wind sprints, followed by BP, and work on his defense. Then it's more stretching, more hitting, before he relaxes with his music. He told *Baseball Digest*, "I don't take anything for granted. Even if I go 4 for 4, I keep coming back to do my routine."

On the physical side of prep, Rickey Henderson gets in wonderful shape by doing pushups with a passion. Although his physique resembles that of a heavy-duty weight lifter, he says he avoids weights. However, when a commercial pops on his TV screen, he plops to the floor for a mini-workout. By the time he's watched a movie on the tube, he's gone through perhaps 500 pushups, normally doing, he says, 50 at a pop. He said that he also works on flexibility rather than sheer strength because he believes weight training can be harmful, often leading to injuries.

Another star who never took to weight lifting is smooth-fielding, hard-hitting Mark Grace. He asserted, "I just feel I'm loose, and my bat's quicker with a 200-pound frame. If it ain't broke, don't fix it."

Meanwhile, sluggers such as Ron Gant, Rob Deer, Mickey Tettleton, Lance Parrish, and Pete Incaviglia were pioneers on the weight-lifting front. These men tended to wallop the ball for power while hitting for low averages and striking out frequently. However, they did play their role and had value, lasting quite some time in the majors.

When baseball's power explosion was in its infancy, back in the pre–70-home-run days, Tettleton, who could pass for a pro wrestler, directly traced the game's home-run outbursts to conditioning and lifting. "I think players are keeping themselves in shape year-round, doing more weight work. Guys are just stronger now. Whenever you get a guy out there throwing hard, and you get a guy swinging hard, you have him hit one, you got a helluva collision."

Lee Smith felt that almost everybody was getting "bigger and stronger now—they don't have to hit the ball on the button to hit it out. Eight out of nine guys are capable of hitting the ball out of the ballpark."

Barry Bonds has, of late, spent much of his spare time working out. His godfather, Willie Mays, admired Bonds's preparation. "He always goes about his business the same way," he said in 2002. "I'm not surprised he's having the success he is, because he's got great talent. But he works hard to use it, too."

Yogi Berra wrote in his book *What Time Is It? You Mean Now?* that today's players pay more attention to exercise than players from his era do. "We only got in shape during spring training, but these guys work out year-round and you can see a difference in their longevity." He felt Bonds went from being a good home-run hitter to a record-setting one due to his training. "He got real serious about it [his health]," Berra wrote, "using a nutritionist and a new workout regimen."

Back in the early 1990s, one clubhouse manager estimated he spent about 85 percent of his $33,000 locker-room budget on the food. Prior to an afternoon game, players typically gulp juices, slurp cereal, nibble on fruit, and even gobble some pastry. Players normally make this a light meal, though.

After the game, it's back to the food table. Baerga listed typical players' eating habits. "We eat lots of salad, chicken, steak, and pork chops." A one-time Cleveland teammate of Baerga, Albert Belle, continued along those lines, "There's a lot of food to choose from. You want nutritious food, it's there. You want junk food, it's there, too. You're gonna want junk food once in awhile, [but] the good thing is we burn it off. Generally, I keep a pretty good diet to try and be in top condition for peak performance." Belle's percentage of body fat was said to be less than 10 during his playing days.

When coach Mike Cubbage was a player, he avoided eating cheaply as some players used to do in order to pocket some of their per-diem money. "I tried never to do that," he said, "because I was thinking of my career and I probably spent more on meals when I was playing than I do now. A lot of the times in the old days the parks just had cold cuts, and a lot of times the food they had after games wasn't exactly what you'd call fine cuisine. Now I can fix a pretty good meal with the clubhouse spread in most cities — not everywhere, but most places I can. You can usually get a decent meal after a game. They also have stuff there for lunch — sandwiches and fruit."

Players truly do put in a lot of time in the off-season nowadays with the focus on nutrition, weight lifting, and other training programs. In fact, Cincinnati star Ken Griffey Sr. started a workout program of his own before he entered the majors, working out on his own on his high school's fields, trimming seconds off his time in various dashes.

As Oakland's Eric Byrnes grew up, he studied martial arts with his dad, Jim. Jim Byrnes is a karate expert who had instruction and workout opportunities with Ed Parker, the man who popularized karate in the United States. Jim knew martial arts would help his son, saying, "It's great for balance, coordination, timing, reaction, and hand speed. It's also of great overall benefit for physical and mental skills." Eric achieved what his dad calls "black-dot focus" — that is, when purpose, passion, and performance come together in knowing that you *will* achieve your goal.

Eric worked out with, and learned a great deal from, several of Jim's friends, including former NFL stars Ronnie Lott, Roger Craig, Keena Turner, and Bubba Parris. Jim said, "Eric and Ronnie used to sit and talk. They'd discuss how to approach the game, whatever the game was, and how to handle situations on and off the field. I think Ronnie was an incredible influence on Eric."

Even after making it to pro ball, his father said that Eric "works out five, six hours a day in addition to baseball. He's always working out with weights or doing a variety of aerobic and yoga exercises."

Jim said Eric has even "hiked up and down Squaw Mountain for four-and-a-half hours. But that's part of his conditioning—it's physical toughness, mental toughness. If [there were such] a sport [as] 'contact baseball,' he'd be your guy."

Some players began training with zeal from childhood on, but that's not true of everyone. In a 2000 interview, White Sox outfielder Jeff Abbott said that while his father did buy him weights, they didn't do much else in terms of training or conditioning. "I just played," he said. "What he always told me was, 'If you work hard enough, I don't think there's anything that can keep you from moving up to college and then pro ball. All you got to do is work hard enough.'

"That's when I realized, 'I'll see what happens if I work hard enough.' But we didn't get a batting cage or anything like that. We just played. We had a lot of games in Georgia, with good weather, a lot of summer ball. We played so many games a year, it was only a matter of time—you play that many games, you're only going to get better."

Some youth training is even more informal than Abbott's was. Herb Perry, a solid hitter, gained fame early on as the University of Florida's quarterback. It helped that he was blessed with a pretty fair running back to hand off the football to in run situations—Emmitt Smith, the NFL's all-time leading rusher.

As for baseball, Perry said his preparation to become a big-league hitter began in early childhood. "I hit more than anybody. Growing up, I hit rocks religiously, every day. We had a rock road with lime rocks and old flint rocks, and I used tobacco sticks, and that was a baseball game to me."

Tobacco sticks were used in areas such as North Carolina. They were long, skinny sticks used in handling string tobacco hung up in barns. Herb said he'd get the sticks and "break them down to the size I needed. They're about an inch square made out of pine. I can remember having to jump on sticks two and three times, putting them up at a 45-degree angle and jump on them just right to break them in the right spot. I was small enough that every now and then I could jump on them two or three times and they still wouldn't break. They'd throw me back in the air. That may be where my knee problems come from," he laughed. "During baseball season, I'd go over and throw rocks up and play games where this weed was a [home run] fence and that weed was a fence. I never struck out."

During the off-season leading into 1984, catcher Chris Bando took part in an unusual training program featuring a grueling aerobics class. Then, during the season he combined weight lifting with further aerobics. "It's especially important to do something extra during the summer," he said. "The easiest time to get out of shape is during the season, when all you do is play baseball, eat, and sleep."

Kirk Gibson's preparation even included his physical appearance. "I like to feel nasty and grubby. I'm not out there to win a beauty contest; I'm out there to be mean and win, not make friends." Once, during pregame, when asked to discuss his memorable homers, the 1988 World Series hero refused, calling such topics "immaterial. I'm just here to win games," he contended. He felt that anything that wasn't focused to that end was fruitless. Gibson then politely excused himself and went back to his workout.

4

Batting Practice

WHEN IT COMES to pregame preparation, the most talked-about aspect has to be batting practice. Today's ballparks have more batting cages than most fans realize, since they are hidden in the bowels of the parks. However, long ago in parks such as Forbes Field or Wrigley Field, the only place to take batting practice was on the field.

Eventually things changed, explained former Boston manager Grady Little. "They developed them later on, like the one they put out [under] the outfield wall at Wrigley; they got one underneath the centerfield stands in Fenway Park. Those kind of amenities were added later [in parks] where they had room to have them."

Mike Cubbage commented, "All these new ballparks have real nice indoor facilities, usually two sets of indoor cages, one for each team. I remember when I played, if it rained we didn't have batting practice simply because there weren't cages to go to. The result of it all is today's hitters get more practice time, get more swings in. There's a lot of extra batting practice. Plus, they'll show up early and hit in the cage. A lot of times they go down there 15 to 20 minutes before a game and take some more swings or take soft toss and hit off the tee. There's definitely more opportunities for today's players as far as batting practice goes."

Hitting in a batting cage used to be something only done by pros. Nowadays that's changed. As a youngster, Eric Byrnes always had the best equipment available. "We bought him a batting cage," said his father Jim. "We were the first on our block, or even town, to own a batting cage and a pitching machine. That was back in Little League."

Hitting into a net prior to a game is definitely a batting routine for players nowadays. Selby said he does this "just to get loose. Sometimes you go in there and hit off the tee for 'feel.' You're trying to work your hands a little bit, and you're trying to get a feel of staying through the ball, and you're not really concerned about how far the ball's going or where it's going. You're really more concerned about a feel and what you feel like in your swing. Sometimes it's just to get loose."

Players may also be working on mechanics and on hitting the ball to various fields while hitting off the tee. In fact, some hitters move the tee to emulate a ball being thrown in tight or outside. Whatever the reason, big leaguers do take soft toss or tee work quite often.

Many hitters, such as Alex Rodriguez, seem to take interminable rounds of batting practice. However, Rod Carew felt that 15 minutes per day was the most a player should take, except for switch hitters who should hit 10 minutes each way per day. In his book *Art and Science of Hitting*, Carew wrote that for the first few minutes he'd stay loose by making contact with fastballs right down the heart of the plate. Then he would "start asking the pitcher to spot the ball. Several inside, several outside, a few high and a few low." Later he'd have his pitcher mix up his pitches so Carew would not know what or where the pitch would be.

Merv Rettenmund likes his players to take BP quite seriously. "That's the only time of the day you work. I mean, that's the only time you can work on your approach and your swing. Once that's over, it's the game. In batting practice you make sure you swing at strikes. You make sure the rotation on the ball is right when you hit it. And you make sure the ball is going to the middle of the field. Batting practice is the time when you don't B.S. [when] doing your cage work. You can't be thinking of this stuff in the game."

Further, it all starts early for diligent hitters. In Bernardo Leonard's book *The Superstar Hitter's Bible*, Gwynn was quoted as saying he began his BP sessions in the off-season on November 1, and for two months he "hit about three days a week with two hundred swings per day." Then, from the start of the New Year through spring training, he would work on increasing "my number of swings from three hundred to about five hundred per day." Finally, just prior to hitting training camp, he avoids using "the batting machines because they have a tendency to make me jump at the ball before it is seen."

All the repeated cuts are instilling the idea of muscle memory. In order to acquire, develop, and perfect new movement of the body one must repeat that motion, just as a student repeats a poem over and over in order to memorize it. It's also true even with an infant repeating the motions needed to walk; and it holds true for the skill of hitting a baseball.

As Rettenmund put it, players must practice certain batting skills in order to be able to have that skill become automatic. He said, "You can't pull something out of your hat in the game when a guy's throwing 95 [mph] if you haven't worked on it."

Big-league hitters still play pepper, and many use the trick of taking batting practice from a pitcher or machine standing closer than the regulation 60-foot, 6-inch distance from home plate. That way, a pitch that traveled at about 75 mph would explode to the plate, seeming more like a 90+ mph pitch; the batter could work on having quick hands in that fashion.

Thus, one way or another, every single day ballplayers cluster around batting cages, ready to hop into the batter's box when it's their turn to hack at some juicy pitches. Although hundreds of hitters take thousands of cuts, many of them, according to experts, don't reap full benefits from this ritual.

Joe Torre, manager of the New York Yankees, observed, "Too many players take BP for hitting home runs instead of hitting the way they're going to hit in the game." Torre feels the practice, in order to be effective, should achieve two goals, and the first is pretty obvious: "You work on your timing," he said.

The second objective is the player should strive to work on *his* game. "Pete Rose was one of the best," Torre believes. "He took BP the way he played. I think that's what BP is for." Torre said that Gwynn fit that same mold when he slapped at the ball and went the opposite way with balls served up during BP. "No question," said Torre. "You get your timing that way."

The popular manager argues that players take too much BP nowadays. He seems to believe that taking fewer swings, but doing so purposefully, would accomplish more.

So just how does Gwynn work on his game? One of his theories is rather unusual: "Never change," said the all-time great during the early 1990s. "Keep it simple. I use a basic approach." Aside from some tinkering, Gwynn, who was an opposite-field hitter even as a kid, said, "I stand in the same spot, use the same bat. I don't move up in the box; I don't move back in the box. My trigger [mechanism] is when the pitcher comes with the pitch, my weight is balanced. Then, like every good hitter, the weight transfer must be crisp. I want to hit the ball to left field, but if they come inside, I have to pull it. The majority of balls I hit do go to left. I'm gonna stick with my strength."

Gwynn admitted, though, that early in his career he'd just get in the box and whack at the ball; later it became an entirely different story. Like the great Ted Williams, Gwynn took batting *and* batting practice seriously, on a higher plane than most hitters did.

It was fascinating to watch Gwynn do his pregame preparation. Prior to a pitch during BP, Gwynn would say to himself or to a nearby teammate, "I'm gonna dump this one to left." Or, if another Padre had just jacked one out, Gwynn might accept a challenge and say, "Guess I have to go deep with this one." Moments later . . . WHACK! . . . and, with seeming ease, he had pulled the ball over the right-field wall.

Gwynn felt that he had to work especially hard in BP prior to facing a knuckleball pitcher since that specialty pitch is what he calls "the one pitch I can't stay back on enough. My swing is geared to guys who throw 80 to 85 mph." He hated, for example, facing knuckleballer Tom Candiotti. Gwynn once said, "Every time I've faced him this year, I've gone in the tank for three days after seeing his knuckler."

Some younger players, having observed men like Gwynn, took a page out of his book. Atlanta's Chipper Jones, for instance, said that he has developed a strict BP routine. He said he mainly works on hitting the ball to certain areas that he has predetermined. During later rounds of practice he also likes to go with the pitch for a few cuts. Finally, he will let loose and try to crank some out of the park. He does this, he says, not to draw the inevitable oohs and ahs from the early-bird spectators, but simply to get loose.

When Manny Ramirez was with Cleveland in 1999, he began the first fourth of that season ablaze. At the end of May, the right fielder had stats that projected to .350, 46 HR, and an impossible 208 RBIs for a full season. (The major-league record is 191.) In addition, at one point late in May he had amassed a staggering 165 RBIs over his previous 139 games!

Ramirez, like Jones, has a definite plan: his first round in the cage features strokes to the opposite field. The next time he takes his cuts, he mainly tries to take the ball up the middle. Even when the other Indians played a game they call "longball," trying to propel deep blows, Ramirez focused instead on line drives.

Chicago Cubs great Ryne Sandberg added, "During batting practice I will envision hitting against that day's pitcher and hit accordingly. If the pitcher is a breaking-ball pitcher, in batting practice I will ask for more breaking balls and balls away. In batting practice I try to hit everything on a line or ground balls."

Players who hit from both sides of the plate have it tough as they must put in many hours to become adept at that skill. Golden Glover Omar Vizquel believes switch hitting has helped his offense immensely. He continues to work on switch hitting, including daily workouts swinging both ways.

In BP, he says, "you do have to keep both [sides] refreshed, because when you do the switch from one hand to another, the swing is not the same. The dominant hand from one side is the opposite of the other one, so it's hard to keep them both together. You always take extra cuts early before batting practice." He has to do that because once BP starts, all regulars get the same amount of cuts. There are no extra swings just because a player happens to be a switch hitter; hitters are very protective about their share of time in the cage.

Clearly, some of the great hitters elect to work on their total game, not just their power game, during BP. For example, despite his astronomical power outputs, Ken Griffey Jr. still insists, "I don't think of myself as a home-run hitter. I like to hit [and focus on] line drives. I just try to hit the ball hard." Dave Winfield, who banged out 3,110 hits, once said something similar: "I'm a line-drive hitter." He would not participate in BP pyrotechnics.

Milwaukee's Richie Sexson said his approach in BP is to use all the fields, to "just work around the field. You start in right field, go to center, then left, and then, by the end of the round, you just hit it where the ball's pitched. You just try to get loose—that's it."

Former Pirate Milt May said that as powerful as Stargell was, "in most cases when I played with Willie, during batting practice he wasn't really trying to hit the ball [far]; he was trying to hit the ball all over, trying to sting the ball. He wasn't really up there grunting and groaning, trying to hit it out of the park. He certainly could've done that; he did during games—he had as much power as anybody did, but that wasn't his game plan. During BP he didn't hit many balls out. He was hitting the ball the other way, trying to get loose, and working on things specifically."

"All of my hitters," said hitting coach Tom McCraw, "if you watch them hit the first round, they hit everything the other [opposite] way. All good hitters do this. To get here and hit those 'five o'clock home runs' doesn't do anything."

Although star outfielder Brian Giles admits that, on occasion, he does try to crank a few home runs when he takes BP, he says he does it as a method to really loosen up his muscles—and partly to please the hometown fans. Just as Pac Bell has McCovey Cove as a crowd-pleasing splashdown target for sluggers, hitters such as Giles have tried in BP to launch a ball entirely out of the park in Pittsburgh and into the Allegheny River beyond right field, even though they realistically understand it takes a miracle of a shot to reach the water. Further, Giles is smart enough to avoid trying to hit home runs constantly in BP or in games.

As McCraw put it, "I never talk about home runs because home runs are a by-product of good hitting, of hitting the ball hard consistently. Once home runs get in the forefront of your mind, I guarantee you that Giles or anybody else stops becoming a good hitter." He said if a player with some punch, for example, tried to go out and shoot for 20 home runs, they might succeed, but they may very well also "hit .240, .250. When you concentrate on being a good hitter, you still are going to hit your 30 to 35 home runs. Only God knows how many home runs you're going to hit."

Rico Carty said he simply tried to hit the ball hard, knowing if he smashed a solid line drive, it might carry for a homer, but he would not try for homers, per se. If he hit the ball well and it didn't leave the park, he might wind up with a productive double, but players who strive for homers sometimes wind up powering a long but harmless ball—one that looks good off the bat, scraping the sky, and impressing the fans, but winding up as a long out.

Fans in Cleveland used to get frustrated with fleet-footed Kenny Lofton when he'd suddenly jack a few balls out of the park, then seemingly fall in love with the long ball, eschewing tactics such as slapping or bunting the ball for safe, albeit short, hits.

McCraw said, "Mentally, you've got to know what you are [e.g., power hitter versus contact hitter] and you've got to know what good hitting is about. I've had guys ask me how to hit home runs. I tell them, 'I don't know how to do that; I know how to teach you to be a good hitter, but that's it.' After that, 20 home runs, 10, or 5—I don't know, but I know what good hitting is."

Al Kaline won a batting crown in only his second full season in the majors, at the age of 20. He was quoted in *The Mike Schmidt Study* as saying, "I think hitters today concentrate too much on hitting the ball out of the ballpark in batting practice. My concentration was on hitting the line drive, reacting with two strikes, reacting to where they were going to pitch me." In other words, he would put himself in game situations to fine-tune his hitting.

Sexson, though, said that for players like Sosa and McGwire, hitting long shots in BP isn't necessarily wrong. "They hit bombs in BP, and they hit them in the game, too—so whatever works."

It should be noted that trying to take a BP pitch for a long ride all the time may not be too smart, but doing so at times can be tempting and fulfilling. After all, players are human beings, and they often crave attention, adulation, or respect.

May, a long-time coach and observer of the game, as well as a player from 1970–84, has seen a lot of batting practice. Normally, BP is a routine event, but several memories of men trying to get loose by heaving long blasts stood out for May. "There was the All-Star game in Pittsburgh (1994), and Ken Griffey [Jr.] hit about six balls in the upper deck in BP. I've been here for years watching batting practice, and just occasionally there's one ball that'll go up there. And he takes BP in the home-run contest and hits about six out of ten up there! That's pretty amazing. He's the only guy I've seen to hit multiple [homers] — he hit like four out of five at one time — I've never seen that done, not close."

He shook his head, remembering that he had seen some impressive hitters try to send balls into those distant regions, only to fail. "I've seen some pretty big guys take a lot of batting practice. I played with Willie Stargell for three years. He hit the ball as far as anybody."

Fans still talk about the time in Toronto when leviathan hitter Cecil Fielder, like Griffey Jr., decided to go for the gusto. Before the '91 All-Star game he got hold of a fat pitch and deposited it in the restaurant that sits in straight-away center, high above the SkyDome field.

Hitting such homers, even during BP, is actually not all that easy. Before a game in 1992 in Tiger Stadium, Mark Carreon bet Fielder that big Cecil could not hit one of the next five offerings for a homer. Fielder scoffed and accepted the wager for a soft drink.

First pitch: nothing. Second pitch: Fielder lifted the ball deep to center, a colossal shot near the 440-foot mark. Fielder barely gave it a glance, as he knew it wasn't close to being out of this particular park. The next two pitches again produced nothing. Final pitch: "All right, here it is," said the home-run artist, but his swing only resulted in another long fly.

Worse, in the home-run contest held prior to the 2003 All-Star game, the amiable Bret Boone had to grin and bear it when he swung and missed on a BP pitch — a far cry from swatting a homer. Thus, if Ted Williams is correct that hitting a baseball is the hardest thing to do in sports, by extension, hitting a baseball for a homer is way more difficult.

Home runs aside, there are players who don't take other phases of BP seriously. The Yankees circa 1977–1981 often put on a dazzling show during batting practice. Players such as Graig Nettles, Reggie Jackson, Thurman Munson, and Chris Chambliss could put a hurt on the baseball. Still, when called upon to lay down a few practice bunts before swinging away, one slugger joked about how he'd never need to bunt in a game, so as Alfred E. Newman might say, "What? Me worry?"

Nettles, for one, would grin, make a perfunctory effort, and then get down to the task he was born for: ripping away at pitches with an interest that matched his ability. Why bother, then, to go through the sham of bunting? Why bother to have a Sosa bunt? Why not give such power hitters several extra cuts in lieu of the bunts?

Francona said that asking a player who may never bunt in the game to lay down a few in a round of BP isn't a waste. "Our guys [in Texas] bunt because, first of all, you *may* bunt in the game, and second, it's a great way to start the day because you see the ball. It all goes back to seeing the ball; you just try to train yourself to get in good habits." Bunting essentially forces a hitter to follow the ball all the way from the pitcher's hand to when it makes contact with the bat.

McCraw commented that the game of baseball has evolved to the point of specialization. "A guy like Sosa, a guy like [Fred] McGriff, a guy like [Vladimir] Guerrero—all your superstuds, [Jason] Giambi, these guys that crush the ball. Sure, you don't want them to bunt, but you want them to have that in their back pocket.

"Now, you say, 'Why? These guys hit home runs and drive in runs.' Because even those guys go into funks. You got a third baseman playing back in the outfield to cut off your base hits and I'm in a funk of 1 for 15 or 1 for 18, why not drop down a bunt and get a base hit? It may get you started. It's not something I'm going to do all the time, but it's something I can pull out of my pocket if I need it. That's the only reason you'd want a guy like that to bunt—when the hits are coming few and far between." The logic is: if the defense is going to give you a hit and you're struggling, take it.

Players such as Rose with his all-time record 4,256 hits, Gwynn and his .338 lifetime average, and Stargell with his 475 home runs had many aspects of hitting in common. For one thing, they all knew the value of taking batting practice properly. As coaches and managers from Little League to the major leagues have said for years, "You play like you practice."

McCraw appreciates such sentiments. He said that what he wants his hitters to achieve in batting practice is simple: "good work habits and work conditions. What is BP?" he asked rhetorically. "Batting practice—so you practice the same things that you're going to have to do in the game, things that you want to do in the game."

He said it ties in with muscle memory. "You're training your muscles to do certain things in certain situations. But the biggest muscle you've got is in your head—you want to train that one most of all. You work on different phases of hitting so that when a situation arises in a ball game, it's not strange to you."

Jim Riggleman was a coach with the Indians in 2000. He said, "I think our guys have a good work ethic in batting practice. They try to stay down on the ball and use the opposite field for several swings in the first round, next use the middle of the diamond, and then the last couple of rounds they might get loose and see how the ball's jumping off their bat. But I think for the most part they're staying pretty much fundamentally sound, trying to drive down and through the ball."

Grady Little said BP, when it's all boiled down, is "all up to the individual. Some guys can stand to not take it at all for a couple of days during this time of year [August] just to give their bodies a moment of relaxation. But there are guys who need to take it religiously, like Tony Gwynn. He doesn't just take your regular BP, he hits earlier everyday and on the road and at home during the season. I was with him in 1996, and I sat there and watched that. But some guys need it a little more than others; some guys may not need it at all some days."

As a hitting coach, Rettenmund wants his players swinging at strikes—naturally. However, he's seen bad habits form during BP. Players who love to take their share of hacks at BP offerings will frequently chase almost any practice pitch, including those out of the strike zone. Very seldom does a hitter take a pitch in the cage.

Rettenmund went on, "It's something that bugs the [expletive] out of me, and it's something that we're [Toronto] going to get back to this year [2003]. Guys take 5,000 swings a year, a day, or a week in baseball now—it's incredible the way these guys work. People think they're lazy. They're not. But how many guys work on the take? You have to do that half the time, too, don't you?

"I guarantee you, if I showed you Barry Bonds on a couple of takes this year, you wouldn't see other players taking a pitch like Barry Bonds does. He takes the ball with a professional take, a real take, with his hands going forward. He's ready to swing: ready, ready, stop. There used to be a comment made, and it sums up what we're going to do this year: 'Great hitters can take their hands way out across their face before they commit to a swing and the umpires don't call it a strike.'

"Remember Frank Robinson? He used to take his hands way out and then stop the swing way out in front. When your hands go across your face, the barrel is still behind your hands, and now all you got left to do is whack the ball. It's like playing pepper because your hands are way out in front, but you haven't swung yet. The guys who do that don't get fooled.

"And a lot of times they dropped the bat. Well, that is an aggressive take—you're in the hitting position. These guys today, these buffoons, they're up there with their hands back behind their head, chasing pitches. They can't hit it from there. I mean, what are they doing? It's like you said, in BP they don't practice taking, so they don't do it in the game, either. They're just up there [ripping]. Everyone practices swinging, swinging, swinging and no one practices taking, taking, taking."

As Rettenmund suggests, it makes sense to take pitches in batting practice. Rose used to work on tracking pitches—he even followed pitches all the way into the catcher's mitt as a matter of routine. However, when most batters are offered a pitch that's not hittable during practice, they have been known to shout angrily at the BP pitcher, "Throw strikes, dammit."

Rettenmund said sarcastically, "I like this one, too, when the hitter turns around and says, 'Where was that pitch?' You say, 'Whose strike zone is it? Mine or yours?' He says, 'Well, it's mine, but was it a strike?' 'Hey,' replies Rettenmund, 'if you don't know if it's a strike, don't bitch at the umpires for making a bad call.' But that's the way the game has changed."

One player who takes pitches particularly well is New York star David Justice (also formerly of Atlanta and Cleveland). He also seems to get away with not getting called for a strike on a checked swing that probably *wasn't* really checked. Rettenmund observed, "I've seen him on TV a few times, and he sure looks like he does [get away with his checked swings]—he gets into the count pretty good, too."

He likened the way the home-plate ump checks with the base ump for help on those close checked swings of Justice to the way they had to check on "Frank [Robinson] a thousand times a year. A lot of guys used to run their hands further out in front, and that's the definition of a short swing." It helps to get the close calls, too, said Rettenmund "if you do it regularly because then it's not a swing [in the umpires' eyes]."

BP can have indirect benefits. Travis Fryman is the kind of player who prepares not only by discussing the game, but also by observing. When he was with the Indians, Fryman said he learned a lot by watching Ramirez. Fryman said, "He prepares himself every day to hit. If you watch Manny in BP, 70 to 80 percent of the balls he hits go to right field [the opposite field]. That's the thing I've really taken from Manny. I've tried to incorporate that into my game."

5

Behind the Scenes: Science, Technology, and Enhancement

NOWADAYS, THE SCIENCE of hitting is, of course, much more sophisticated than it was during the "hit 'em where they ain't" era. From club "videographers," a term that would probably make Ty Cobb retch, to a legion of computerized hitting aids, and to the realm of sport psychology, there is more help available today to hitters than ever before.

Dr. Charles Maher, the sport psychologist and director of psychological services for the Cleveland Indians, is responsible for the mental skills and performance enhancement of all Cleveland players as well as mental testing for their annual amateur draft. One technique Dr. Maher employs with Indians players is known as visualization. It's a method that ties in with the concept of muscle memory, in which a player pictures a scenario in his mind—a scenario in which the batter succeeds. Therefore, if a hitter is to face, for example, the Yankees' Mike Mussina, he might sit quietly, almost meditatively, picturing Mussina's delivery, his release point, and the ball approaching the plate. Then, to top things off, he may imagine himself drilling a line-drive single with a runner in scoring position—

or, if his imagination is particularly vivid and his confidence high, he may "see" a home run sailing off his bat and into a throng of screaming fans.

Former big leaguer Willie Upshaw said, "All good players do it to a certain extent. When you see enough pitches [and store them in your mind], that's a form of visualization. When you're at the plate, all you have time to do is react to the ball; your visualization takes over."

For a hitter, recognizing pitches boils down to "a lot of repetition with good technique. They're getting visualization whether they know it or not—you can't hit a Roger Clemens without knowing where the ball is going to go [based on previous at-bats and a good memory]."

Some hitters take visualization to a higher plane, almost a "yoga-type thing. Some players do that; you'll see a guy with his eyes closed sitting at his locker after BP—he's not taking a nap!" Upshaw said many of those hitters are using the technique when they are in the dugout studying the opposing pitcher and even when they gaze out at the pitcher on the mound as they take warm-up cuts from the on-deck circle. "In their mind they're timing the pitcher." Some will actually swing the bat, others are "taking [timing] cuts in their mind."

Ed Spiezio trained his son Scott in such techniques. First, Ed would set up imaginary game conditions for his son. The former big leaguer would throw pitches to various spots, moving the ball around just as pitchers do. In other words, Ed would try to emulate the thought process of a big-league hitter, trying to set his son up when he threw BP to Scott. That gave him a glimpse into the world of the big leagues, into the minds of pitchers.

Ed said that when he was a kid he'd always imagine that it was up to him to take a last-second, game-winning shot in basketball. As a father, he'd set up similar baseball conditions with Scott. "Two down," he would instruct the budding star. "You're up with a chance to win the ball game with a guy on third base—gotta drive him in."

Scott has been a proponent of visualization perhaps longer than any other player, since he began using this technique almost from infancy. When Scott hit a key three-run homer in Game 6 of the 2003 World Series with the Angels down 5–0 and just a few innings away from elimination, he felt he (and his father) had prepared himself for this crucial at-bat many times in the past. "I feel like I've been in a thousand postseason games," he told *USA Today Sports Weekly*. "We visualized this kind of thing so many times."

Ed's logic had been sound: he tried to put Scott in tough, albeit artificial, spots so that when he faced the real moment it would be no big deal. Sure enough, moments prior to his comeback-sparking home run, Scott said he was thinking "about being in the backyard, thinking about having a good at-bat."

Scott says he likes to go over the feeling of solid contact in his mind as part of his visualization. To help him do this, he turns his brain into a video recorder and immediately stores good at-bats away for future use. While he said his mental approach and techniques are quite elaborate, and can occur anywhere from the dugout to the on-deck circle to, of course, his old backyard, when he was at bat for his World Series homer, he kept thinking of simple things such as getting the bat head out and just making contact if he didn't get a pitch he could drive.

Not everyone agrees with the Spiezios regarding visualization. Rickey Henderson grinned at the thought of relying on visualization, hypnosis, or other forms of mind over batter, saying, "I try not to do that. I know some guys who have scientists come in and try to help them adjust to the game and make their minds relaxed, focused on what they're trying to do. That's just [for] certain people that need that; I didn't need that. I always loved the game, and I didn't put stress on myself to say, 'I *gotta* have success.'"

Moving from psychology to technology, Bob Chester is the manager of video operations for the Cleveland Indians, an organization that not only enjoyed a long stretch of success in the 1990s, but also one that bought into the viability and the power of technology in baseball early on. When they began in the early 1980s, they were still using black-and-white cameras. "Back then," said Chester, "the system consisted of shooting the players' at-bats with a hand-held camera. And when the team was on the road, they just popped tapes into a VCR when the games were televised." They'd have different tapes for each hitter and would have to put a tape in with each batter change during the contest.

His duties now, he said, are "to assist the team in all video-related aspects that pertain to video coaching, game analysis, advance scouting, player acquisition as far as free agency and draft selections go. What we do is provide edited and cut-up tapes of potential free agents, and we go through some of our draft selections, depending upon what's requested of us from the front office."

The benefits of such technology for the hitting coach and the hitters are enormous. Coaches scrutinize tape for items such as body mechanics and, says Chester, "Hitting coaches will also help a player look at pitchers' tendencies."

Individual hitters often come to Chester requesting a CD be burned for them with specific footage included. "Right now we're in the process of finalizing a lot of our end-of-season tapes and CDs," Chester said. "We're now into DVD mode, where we've gotten various requests from players, some more specific than others. Some guys just want to see everything from the entire year — of course this is all edited down pitch-by-pitch — but some guys want to see maybe just the positive aspects." Whatever they want to see, it's there; every at-bat for every player is captured.

Chester has worked with some superstars of the game who used technology to varying degrees. Chester began, "Manny Ramirez was a player who utilized the video department just as he would any other portion of his game in preparing for a particular game. He would come in for a prescribed amount of time — maybe five, ten minutes — and look at the opposing pitcher — past performances versus himself against that pitcher. And he would basically write down what types of pitches were thrown at him. It could have been two or three different outings of that pitcher, and he would log all the stuff down.

"Albert Belle was similar to that, too, and they would reference that information. Belle would use it more to see the pitcher and if he was tipping pitches by looking at the glove, the angle of the glove, things like that. Robbie Alomar tended to do the same type of thing."

Belle was so much into the study of video that the moody slugger said he tended to stay after a game and "maybe watch videos of opposing pitchers [for the next game], or watch my at-bats. You see how you're hitting when you're going good or going bad, and you can make corrections." Belle said he learned a great deal from watching videotapes that displayed the contrast between his hitting when he was hot and the occasions when he was in a funk.

He would also study tape of the opposing pitcher on game days. "The more you see a pitcher, the more confident you are," he stated. Then, before a Cleveland versus Seattle game, he gave an example. "Today we're facing Brian Fisher, so we have a tape of his last outing against us. You get a picture of how he'll face us today. We also have all of our at-bats on tape."

There's no doubt that technology helps. For instance, Matt Williams, then an Indian, once worked under hitting coach Charlie Manuel. During one session, Brian Giles was, said Chester, "sitting in, watching, and Williams at the time was struggling. They were going over some adjustments that he needed to make.

"Then, after he was finished, Manuel talked to Brian and asked, 'Would you like to see your last time that you faced [that night's starting pitcher]?' Brian said sure, and Charlie popped a tape in and they noticed that Brian needed to adjust his stance, and he did. That's the beauty of video: you look at what you need to do, go to the hitting cages, practice that there pregame, and then that particular night I remember he went 2 for 3, and you know that there was a positive correlation."

Upshaw added that technological advances have reached down into the minor leagues as "the kids today even look at video now," an advantage he didn't have during his climb to the majors.

A few years ago, Padres coach Rob Picciolo stressed the value of video but offered a word of caution. "Every pitch now is recorded on video; you can watch every swing and every pitch. I think sometimes that's helpful and sometimes it's detrimental to players. You can overdo it with that stuff.

"You know, Tony Gwynn was a big advocate of it, and Tony used it, I think, the correct way. I think it's more advantageous for players to look at good swings than look at bad swings. Reinforce in their mind the good swing rather than the bad swing."

Indeed, Gwynn was one of the first famous hitters to study video diligently, almost endlessly. He had his own portable video machine that he watched for more hours than the average Neilsen viewer sits comatose in front of the tube. Gwynn's goal was to understand his craft. If he went on a tear, he wanted to know why. A rare slump? Back to the video for Gwynn. More homework.

As recently as 1996 Gwynn was lugging two VCRs on the road. He'd record his game with one and transfer each at-bat with the other. He'd then sort his plate appearances into his good at-bats, those that produced hits, and the swings that led to outs as well. According to *USA Today*, in the 1980s he was practically his own video department, carrying 11 cassettes with him on road trips so he could study his every at-bat against each National League club. So studious was he, his wife said he once watched an individual at-bat 100 times.

In Cleveland, Bob Chester's video equipment is in the clubhouse, "right across from the locker room. We have a logging system—a baseball nonlinear 'editor' is what they call it (with no physical cutting or splicing). It's all computerized, so we're literally logging every pitch of every game whether it's home or away and labeling not only balls and strikes but position, where the ball was thrown, what type of pitch it was, and then the result of the at-bat, exactly where it was hit and how it was hit. That information, by the time the game is over, creates a large database, so that way you can go to any point in the game and call up that play instantly, since it's on a computer and it's random access.

"We also have field cameras that are robotic, and we can position those to focus on whatever a coach may want us to for a particular game. A lot of times hitters want profile angles [of their at-bats] on their open side so they can take a look at what they're doing and make adjustments."

Some players make use of the technology during games. They'll take the trek from the dugout, up the runway, and into the video area to study an at-bat. Chester said, "A player can take a look at any sequence of pitches and how the pitcher threw at any point during the game. All teams have systems where a player can take a look during the game. It's not like the NFL where coaching staffs aren't allowed to look at video at halftime. Baseball's different; obviously you can't have anything in the dugout, but you can have equipment in the confines of the clubhouse."

So, if a hitter makes an out and wants to watch how the pitcher had just worked him, he can watch the tape immediately. Likewise, some designated hitters can view that day's opposing pitcher by watching the clubhouse television during the game.

Even when a team is on the road, Chester said that "they bring their own video equipment in, somewhere behind the bat-swing area, fairly close to the dugout, and we [the Indians at home] have a similar area here which isn't too far for a player to have to go. Then again, when you go on the road, depending on where you are and how the ballpark is situated, they may have quite a distance to go. In those instances, you may only get a DH to come by every now and then or a pitcher to take a look. The other guys just don't have the time." Naturally, if either team is going to have an advantage, it's the home team in a park configured for their convenience, not the other team.

The Indians, among others, also make use of a state-of-the-art pitching machine that enables players, said Chester, "to plug in a particular pitcher, and it's supposed to emulate the break on their ball or the speed and location of their fastball. I talked to some of the players a couple of years ago during spring training when we were first looking at it, and it's one of those things—either the players love it or feel like it's just a gimmick. And it doesn't really matter whether they're a younger player or an older one.

"Some guys felt, 'Yeah, that was really a good way for me to work on hitting this particular pitcher's breaking ball, and I think it will help.' Other players say, 'I really don't look at it that way. It won't be a help at all.' So, it's on an individual basis."

Upshaw also discussed the machine. "It's like facing a major-league pitcher off a video game or live. You can program it [to do almost anything a pitcher does]—it's very sophisticated. It's about as close to [facing] the real thing as you can get without a real guy up there." Thus, many of the batters who love the machine feel it emulates game conditions a lot better than facing, for instance, a coach lobbing balls during batting practice.

Picciolo agreed that when he had seen it demonstrated, it seemed like "it's as close to, as realistic to, a game situation as you can get." He continued, saying that a good swing comes from more than taking BP against a fantastic machine. "Basically [hitting] is a 'feel'. Alan Trammell has always said that it's a feel you have to have. There's a lot that goes into a swing, but there is also a sense of confidence—he calls it feeling 'hitterish,' and I agree with that. That's what the good hitters do." When Colorado's Todd Helton hit three homers in a 2003 contest, he announced, "Hitting for me is definitely a feel thing."

In addition, John McDonald is one of the Indians' players who does not use the modern machine, not because he doesn't like it, but because, he said, "I have my own ways to get ready, get loose for the game. You work your whole way up [to the majors] doing one thing, and just because you get here you shouldn't [necessarily] change."

He did, though, appreciate the machine's uniqueness. "It fabricates a pitcher out on the mound throwing pitches, different kinds of pitches out of the machine." The $150,000 machine does, in fact, mimic the speed, spin, and break of big-league pitchers. It even makes the ball seem as if it's coming out of the hand of a computer-made pitcher projected onto a video screen.

The Mariners have a machine that propels tennis balls at 150 mph. Edgar Martinez, arguably the finest DH in baseball history, swears by this tool, bunting against it to help his hand-eye coordination. Then he'll slow the speed down and try to read the numbers placed on the balls as they rip by him. He told *Sports Illustrated*, "After tracking a smaller [tennis] ball going 150 miles an hour, a baseball going 90 doesn't seem so fast." It's the same principle as taking practice cuts with a weighted bat before entering the batter's box.

Another and much older machine is the radar gun, which is used to help make reports and evaluations. Many teams have an employee situated behind home plate in the stands armed with one of these guns. The most famous such person is probably Mike Brito, the Los Angeles Dodgers scout who discovered Fernando Valenzuela and signed him to a Dodgers contract. Brito is the man who stands out from the crowd when seen on television not merely because he is holding the radar gun, but also because of his distinctive cigar and white Panama hat.

In Cleveland, Todd Harris manned the gun during the 2002 season and worked on charts. He explained his duties and how his work helps Cleveland players. "I chart every pitch—the velocity and what type of pitch it was. For each pitch, I mark if it was a ball or a strike, so I do everything except location, which I do the following day while watching the game again on a computer. I have a VCR hooked up to my computer. Our video department tapes our games for us and I take it from there [making my report].

"A lot of what I'm doing ties in to our advance scouting reports and also for data for the front office to look at and evaluate. It's a way to see trends. We put the information in the computer and see things like if batters are having success against pitches in certain locations." That is to say, they look for a "hot zone."

"We're building up a huge storehouse of information. If a certain player was struggling, we could look at the data. It's not a constant evaluation, but if we saw something [that would help a hitter], we'd see if the computer had the data to verify what we saw. First and foremost we rely on the coaching staff and what they notice, but sometimes it's interesting to look at the data as well." Thus, there's still much to be said about the importance of the naked eye of a veteran coach in determining problems with hitters' mechanics.

To prepare for upcoming opponents, the Indians don't use the typical scout who has been around baseball forever and always stays one city in front of the team. "It's all in-house now," said Harris. "We do have pro scouts on the road, but they're watching for future acquisitions. For advance scouting, it's all in-house. We have an advance scout here in Cleveland who talks often with those pro scouts [who are out on the road] in case they have recently seen upcoming opponents."

Harris added that they can record most of the major-league games played in a season. Armed with such information, the Indians will look at an upcoming opponents' last five games, studying their starting pitching rotation and, most likely, the majority of their relievers and maybe even their closer. In fact, even if a team hadn't used their closer just prior to facing the Indians, the team always has recent data on any regular player, one whom the Indians are apt to see, including, of course, their closer.

A specific example of how advance scouting helps, says Harris, is that he "can look at all the information about our batters versus righties or lefties. I can also narrow it down to, say, Roger Clemens versus Indians right-handers to see how Roger attacks those hitters.

"To take those criteria further, I can see Clemens versus righties with two strikes on them to see patterns. How does he like to finish hitters off? Does he like to go to his split finger to make them chase pitches down in the dirt to put them away or does he try to elevate his fastball? Or, with men in scoring position, in tight spots, he may tend to go with his slider, for example.

"Of course, a good pitcher like Clemens will use all of his weapons. The good pitchers are the toughest ones to find a pattern on. It's not an exact science, but we try to give our players even a small advantage."

Another part of the behind-the-scenes athletic enhancement that fans don't get to see is the daily routine of taking care of one's body. One way dedicated players go about that is simple: they watch what they eat.

On game day many players eat a meal about three to four hours prior to the first pitch; they usually eat lightly. Pancakes, pasta, and fruit are commonly found in their diets (while fats and proteins are usually avoided). The most popular drinks tend to be water and sports drinks including Gatorade and Powerade.

At four o'clock prior to a 7:05 start, Michael Barrett was sipping hot coffee in his dugout. When told that Yastrzemski used to drink what seemed like carafe after carafe of coffee before games to become alert, Barrett listened as he gazed out at a few of his teammates stretching. When asked why he drank pregame coffee even on a hot day, he replied, "It's because I like coffee." Seriously, though, like an early morning commuter getting a coffee rush prior to rush hour, there are those players who do enjoy, even crave, the caffeine jolt.

Rickey Henderson said that, unlike those who use coffee to give them a bracer, coffee puts him to sleep. "I'm the opposite," he laughed. "But running, getting oxygen out there, that's what wakes me up."

Unfortunately, there is another type of jolt lately associated with players: the use of illegal substances, the most notorious being anabolic steroids. Back in August 1998, some time before the steroid controversy begun by Ken Caminiti, Mark McGwire told the media that he was using androstenedione, a strength enhancer. He said, "It's legal stuff. . . . Everybody that I know in the game of baseball uses the same stuff I use."

Back then, Tigers General Manager Randy Smith also estimated that steroid use was perhaps as high as 30 percent among position players. Furthermore, Bob Nightengale quoted Padres GM Kevin Towers as saying there were numerous players "using supplements and creatine and everything else, but it's hard to know just how many of those guys are on steroids. I would say there's at least two or three guys on every team, but beyond that, no one knows."

When Caminiti blew the whistle on steroid use, it created a furor. Estimates of the percentage of players using steroids have varied, but in any case, they have sullied some hitting accomplishments.

In the June 3, 2002, issue of *Sports Illustrated*, Jose Canseco put the percentage of steroid users at around 85. In that same issue, Caminiti, who copped the 1996 MVP trophy while on steroids, said it used to be that someone seeking steroids would have to scurry about seeking a black-market source, perhaps in a place like Tijuana, where he first got the substance. "Now," he added, "it's everywhere. It's very easy to get." The article even quoted commissioner Bud Selig as saying, "No one denies that it is a problem."

Caminiti was also quoted in the magazine as saying the players "talk about it. They joke about it with each other." It was, he said pointedly, "no secret what's going on in baseball."

Part of the reason players seek enhancement is the juvenile "the other kids are doing it" argument. Caminiti said that a young guy, out to make a lot of money in the game, might be tempted to use steroids because if he didn't, there were certainly others who would. And those players would take jobs away from the ones who stayed within the letter of the law.

He explained that the use of steroids meant the baseball would travel a bit farther. "Some of the balls that would normally go to the warning track will go out," he confirmed. And that, apparently, is enough of an edge for many players.

Some critics have tried to take away credit from Bonds's accomplishments by bringing up accusations of steroid use. Bonds was said to have countered such accusations by pointing out that he bulked up by undertaking an off-season workout that ran about five hours daily.

In a piece about Bonds, Skip Bayless of Knight Ridder Newspapers pointed out that in 1998 when McGwire hit 70 homers and Sosa swatted 66, Bonds hit only 37. He followed that with a career-high 49 in 2000 before suddenly exploding for 73 the next season. Bayless quoted Dr. Joey Antonio as saying, "Unless you're a genetic freak, it's impossible to put on more than about five pounds of muscle a year without using steroids." He further offered that after the age of 30, it becomes even more difficult to bulk up. Bayless wrote that "several doctors and bodybuilding experts" said that they felt Bonds's "muscle-mass explosion had to be steroid-fueled." The experts argued that Bonds's "face exhibits the puffiness of a man who cycles steroids."

Former teammate Ellis Burks further defended Bonds by pointing out that he's always been a superb hitter. Burks said guardedly, "I'm not one to say who ever did steroids or whatever, but this guy [produced] from day one and he's still doing it. He's a professional hitter; he's a great hitter and he's the man." What separates Bonds from the rest of the crowd, said Burks succinctly is "raw ability."

Clearly, some great hitters were not big on bodybuilding. Former Red Sox player and manager Butch Hobson believes that Boston outfielder Jim Rice was impressively strong because he "was naturally strong. He never used weights or anything. He was [just a] big man." By the same token, Mickey Mantle was far from being a weight-lifting fanatic. Still, fellow Yankee Billy Martin contended that nobody "in the history of baseball had as much power as Mantle. No man!"

Gregg Jefferies, who ended his fine career with the Tigers, said that not too long ago players would come into training camp out of shape. They'd work on fitness during the spring. Now players come to camp in great condition, having worked out all winter.

He also says it's a given that today's players are much bigger and stronger than ever before. "It's nothing seeing a shortstop who's 6'3" that hits 40 home runs like A-Rod [Alex Rodriguez] or Nomar Garciaparra, even [Derek] Jeter." He said that even catchers are no longer hulking types, but seemingly have the dexterity of infielders. He cited men like "the Mike Lieberthals, 'Pudge' [Ivan Rodriguez], Brad Ausmus, Charles Johnson, Jason Kendall."

He doesn't believe that the baseball is charged; instead he says the players are juiced. They hit the weight room so much, they could pass for bodybuilders rather than baseball stars.

Weight lifting is obviously an enormous part of today's baseball scene. Starting around the late 1980s or early 1990s, players such as former Tina Turner bodyguard Lance Parrish, Canseco, McGwire, and many others began to bulk up. Balls began to fly out of parks at a greater rate than they had even during the infamous, explosive 1930 season, "The Year of the Rabbit Ball."

Prior to such pioneers of pumping iron, weight lifting was frowned upon in baseball. Further, little was known about effective weight training. However, successful hitting, resulting in part from lifting, begets more proponents of the use of weights. Tettleton, who possessed a Mr. Olympia physique, said, "I've always lifted weights, but I didn't carry it into the season. Now I do." When a McGwire and a Bonds come along, shattering home-run records while espousing the benefits of weight training, the copycats are bound to follow.

6

Adjustments

ONE REASON THAT hitters must make adjustments is because that's exactly what the pitchers are doing throughout an at-bat, a game, a season, and even over a career. In a 2000 interview, Darin Erstad spoke of how a pitcher will attack a hitter differently late in the game versus earlier. "Sometimes if a pitcher is getting you out, he'll probably try to get you out the same way. If you get hits early, he'll change the pattern on you, no question."

It can become a coy dance. For example, there will be times a pitcher might tell the media a bit of information on how he pitches a certain hitter because, says Erstad, "He hopes we'll hear it [and fall for it]." In other words, it's all a ploy on the part of a cunning pitcher, and hitters must adjust to anything pitchers throw at them—even duplicity.

By 1991 Kevin Maas had displayed some home-run punch in his bat. Because of that, he said he soon noticed the opponents were "pitching me more carefully. They know I can put the ball over the fence on one pitch. A lot of situations that were fastball situations, I'm now seeing off-speed pitches and the ball away from me."

In a 6–0 contest with nobody on base and a full count to Maas, he was surprised at what they threw him. "I've seen breaking balls. It's constant adjusting to how they're pitching you. I adjust to them and hurt them that way." Eventually, the pitchers won this battle as Maas's home-run totals nose-dived from a personal high of 23 to 11, 9, 1, and then ultimately he was gone from the majors after only five seasons.

Next are the changes that take place as hitters mature over the years. Generally, seasoned hitters win more than their share of encounters with the pitchers. Even though some people once considered Ryan Klesko to be a pure power hitter, he has come a long way from his early days—becoming a more complete player and a deeper thinker. He has paid his dues, put in his time, and learned his craft. Some young, strong hitters simply swing from the heels, with no real clue or true insights about hitting. Klesko is much more than just a dead pull hitter, an all-or-nothing swinger.

As for the argument that a pull hitter does not need to use the entire field, that he can be successful by pulling enough balls for numerous crowd-pleasing homers, Klesko prefaced his thoughts by saying, "It depends on where you stand on the plate and how quick you are. I've [had times] in my career where I've been off the plate, and later in my career I'm more on the plate. I like letting the ball get deep a little bit, and I feel that my swing is shorter so I can allow the ball to get deeper, and I'm quicker."

He then went on to say, "But you definitely can't just be a straight pull-the-ball hitter for the most part if you're going to hit for average. Most guys don't use line-to-line [using the entire field], but it's left-center to right-center for most of the power hitters who hit for average. They're using the gaps. They're not necessarily hitting the ball out to left; they're driving from left-center to right-center, using about three-quarters of the field."

Eddie Mathews, who compiled over 500 homers, said that as a youngster he began to do the opposite of what Klesko spoke of. Mathews was drawn to the pure, pull-the-ball, power game, learning how to be a dead pull-ball slugger due to his mother's influence. When he was a boy, his mother threw batting practice to him; he soon discovered that the best way to avoid hitting her, and incurring parental wrath, was to pull the ball.

Andres Galarraga addressed the idea of making changes from one at-bat to another in the same contest. He says he's done that because "some guys throw hard, some throw a lot of breaking balls. So you have to make adjustments for every pitcher and the way that he pitches—slow or fast, in and out. It's just little things you have to concentrate on and adjust [to]." Selby, who is listed at 5′ 9″, commented, "Some guys move around. Since I'm shorter, my limbs are shorter. I'll move up in the box sometimes if a guy's got more movement, so I try to catch balls before they break too much, or it might depend on the strike zone that day. I don't move too much, because if you start moving too much, then the ball gets on you a little quicker and you lose your sense of the strike zone. But you definitely make adjustments in the batter's box."

There are exceptions to almost every rule, and Al Bumbry, who enjoyed a fine big-league career, is certainly one. As a player, he wasn't big on making adjustments. Now, as a coach, he comments, "Let's put it this way: I think I'm more aware of the necessity to make adjustments and changes every at-bat—I'm more aware now than I was when I played. I mean, there were adjustments I think I made off of pitchers and, of course, I think there were ones I made when I had an idea of what the pitcher was trying to do to me when I was at the plate. But overall I can't say that I consciously had that in mind every time I went to the plate."

As he became older, he adapted more. "I became more aware as I played in ball games [over the seasons] in terms of what things I needed to do, and I felt that I made some adjustments. But even today, I look back on my career and I don't think I made as many adjustments as I notice [now] that needed to be made."

Many players make a simple adjustment to age: they ask for days off. That often holds true for hitters dodging day games following night contests. However, in Bumbry's case that was one change he avoided. "I never thought too much about taking days off," he laughed. "I never felt like I needed a day off. I never asked for a day off, and if the manager gave me one, obviously I didn't have any choice in the matter. Of course, a lot of times the manager gives you days and you don't want them, but I would think in terms of preservation, in terms of trying to keep guys fresh physically and mentally, that you need a day off here and there.

"Of course, the other thing is my bat was not as heavy. I went to a lighter bat because as you get older, some of your skills tend to deteriorate. You're not as quick as you were so, obviously, a lighter bat will compensate for the deterioration of some of your reflexes. There are multiple things you do to make adjustments based on your age and your career."

Rickey Henderson observed of the long, tiring season, "You get a little more sluggish, but sometimes I try to train myself. I'm really more the type of guy who tries to make sure his body is trained during the course of a season and, mainly, the whole year round. My body feels different when it's not in shape. I feel sluggish. Once I feel sluggish, I do some running, I try to get some wind, and stuff like that—that's what makes me feel good. I think a lot of people feel better when they're running."

Most fans think of adjustments in terms of a batter adjusting to a pitcher or vice versa, but there's more to it. A player also has to make allowances for the home-plate umpire and his strike zone every single game. Recently, major-league baseball decided to consolidate all its umpires into one group. No longer would there be umps that worked American League games exclusively or umps that were always National League umpires. That helps since there was a marked difference in the styles of the two leagues' umpiring, so batters (and pitchers) had to learn new strike zones.

Picciolo was coaching with the Padres when the change occurred. He noted, "It was an adjustment all players had to make. They also raised the strike zone and it took a while to adjust to that, but I think it still has a lot to do with individuality of the umpire—whether it [his zone] is tight, whether it's big, whether it's up, whether it's down. And I think that's just the human element. Baseball [doesn't use] instant replay and those types of things, . . . so the human element is still a major part of it, and you have to deal with it."

Houston's Jeff Bagwell continued, "It's all under one roof now," he began, "and, yeah, it is tough because you don't know the umpires. But that's what they give us, and that's what you have to work with night in and night out. As long as they're consistent in what they're doing, we're OK."

What can a player do, however, when he faces a rookie umpire, fresh up from the minors, for the first time? Is it trial and error until one learns how to read the ump? Picciolo said the teams don't have any empirical data on new umpires unless "maybe a coach or someone on the team will know that he umpired in the minor leagues, so we'll talk about his strike zone, and talk about how he works, and what his strengths and weaknesses are. Then, you basically find out for yourself. After watching an umpire for a few games, you watch his technique, the way he goes about his business.

"But, usually, when you get a new umpire, someone has seen him along the way—someone [from] the Pacific Coast League or an A-ball league or a Double-A league. I mean, you'll have a little indication of what he's going to be like. It helps."

Similarly, even established players who get swapped to the other league find themselves languishing in the new environment for some time. It takes them a while to get used to their new league. When they finally do get accustomed to their surroundings, their offensive output inevitably climbs. Once they start to know the pitchers, they feel more comfortable. They also must learn the new parks and even what pitches they'll see in the league. For years the National League was known as a fastball league while the American League was known more for curves and its finesse style on certain counts.

When Jim Thome left the Indians to join the Phillies, signing on as a free agent in November 2002, his new manager, Larry Bowa, anticipated Thome would have no trouble acclimating himself to NL pitchers. "If you can hit, you can hit," said Bowa. "We could send him tapes of every pitcher in the National League. He's a baseball player. He prepares."

Some adjustments are made in-game as part of a teamwide ongoing process to win the game. For instance, Coach Picciolo said that major-league players most certainly do share information with their teammates after they've faced a given pitcher—just as kids on sandlots and in high schools have always done. "In high school and college, sure. And college has gotten so advanced now, they have their scouting reports on other players and other teams so you find out, hopefully before the game starts, how this pitcher likes to work, what his out pitch is, and how fast his fastball is.

"If you're a good coach of a high school team, by the time you go around the first couple of innings, word has spread throughout the dugout of how the pitcher throws and what his velocity is, what his out pitch is, and [more info, such as whether] his slider breaks late and when he'll throw his change-up. So there is a lot of charting that goes on now, more so than when I was in college or high school. They chart not only the pitcher, but the opposing hitter [for] where they have a tendency to hit the ball so that you can be more educated and eliminate the element of surprise there may be in the game."

In pro baseball, all players generally have a good idea of what each pitcher throws and how the batters hit, but the sharing of game information is still vital. During a 2002 interview Picciolo confirmed, "The hitters are always talking among themselves, and Duane Espy, our [Padres] hitting instructor, is always sharing information with the hitters on a pitcher. If he hasn't seen a pitcher before, by the time he's gone through the lineup once, Duane has a pretty good idea how he's working, what he's trying to do, what his out pitch is, what side of the plate he likes to work more than the other, and on what counts he'll work certain parts of the plate. There is constant talk and chatter in the dugout about an opposing pitcher."

"Oh, for sure," said Scott Pose. "They'll say, 'What's he got today?' It's more so 'What's the umpire calling today?' Is he giving the pitcher a little more than [usual]? You get general feels like that. Not everybody sees the pitchers the same way, so you say, 'Yeah, he's got a sinker today,' but you can't tell him exactly how much it's moving 'cause it might not look like that to somebody who's hot versus somebody who isn't. So you're just basically coming back to the dugout saying what he's got, and you can see the sequences from the bench. Then, if anybody wants to get more specific, you go ask the guy what he saw."

Fans might think that the leadoff hitter of the game or inning plays the role of the intelligence agent, returning to the dugout with a report on the pitcher, and that can be the case. However, Pose said that's not always true. "No, it's for anybody that comes through [the lineup], especially if you're hitting lower in the order and you hit left-handed and somebody in the upper part of the order is hitting left-handed. [You'd ask him,] 'So, how'd he work you?' You kind of go into it that way."

Years ago, Ken Griffey Jr. said that when he returned to the dugout, he made it a point *not* to tell his teammates what he had seen and how he was being pitched. He wasn't playing the part of a prima donna, but rather felt his input might harm his teammates rather than help. For one thing, he realized that he'd be pitched differently than the other hitters in the lineup. He was convinced there was nothing he could say to benefit the team, that perhaps his advice might even be misinformation.

Upon hearing the Griffey anecdote, Picciolo, who had spent a lot of time around Gwynn in San Diego, related this story: "One guy who comes to mind as a coach is Gwynn. He picks up things after one at-bat on a pitcher, and he shares that information and his hitting philosophies. Tony was always receptive to help anyone. He didn't push himself on other hitters, but if they were open to his ideas and his techniques and his thoughts, then Tony was more than willing to share information with anybody that was willing to listen."

As a leadoff hitter, Johnny Damon not only tries to see a lot of pitches, especially in his first at-bat, but he also plays the spy role, trying to gather information for teammates. "I think you have to let the guys know," he said, "because pitchers change from start to start sometimes, and pitchers change from the start of the season to the end of the season. Their arms get tired, and they don't quite have the leg strength. So I definitely take everything into consideration and let the other players know what's going on."

John Kruk said his 1993 Phillies received such help from their feisty leadoff hitter, Lenny Dykstra. The team felt Dykstra was a true catalyst, and Kruk said, "By the time Lenny was done batting [to start the contest], we had seen all of the pitcher's pitches."

Pitcher Paul Shuey said the Cleveland Indians of the successful 1995–2000 era were good about sharing information on the pitchers that they faced. He said, "Not everybody works that way, but there are a select few guys who do communicate. I know in the past, Robbie [Alomar], Kenny [Lofton], Sandy [Alomar], and Travis [Fryman did]. The tighter the unit you have on the team, the more they say, 'Look, the guy's got a good split,' or something like that. Or, 'What'd you strike out on?' They're not so angry with themselves for striking out, they're more just, 'Look, this is what [he got me on]. Don't swing at it.' So they try to give each other help."

He added that some hitters don't want such information, so they simply stay out of such conversations. However, many hitters, such as Roberto Alomar, will harvest and dissect all the input they can get.

Some hitters ask pitchers on their team for advice. Kenny Rogers, one of an elite group of pitchers to throw a perfect game, said young hitters often come to him to glean insights about the art of pitching in an effort to improve themselves as batters. "I think it doesn't matter [what position a player plays], pitchers can learn from hitters just like hitters can learn from pitchers. You try and pick their brain just to find out what they might do in certain situations—what pitch they might like to throw."

Rogers felt that such a thirst for knowledge is not limited to youth, either. Not only did he continue to seek out advice well into his 30's, he added, "I think good hitters do the same thing." He cited a fundamental of pitching that could benefit a batter if he could look at a facet of pitching from a different frame of reference. A pitcher should be just that, a pitcher, not someone who tries "to throw the ball and overpower a hitter. [A pitcher should] stay in control and not get out of [his] comfort level or comfort zone. [And it's] the same thing for a hitter. Try and swing too hard, try and pull the ball too much, and you're going to get yourself out most of the time."

Since hitters typically gear up to hit the fastball, sometimes they must work diligently to cope with other pitches, too. For instance, Galarraga conceded that knuckleball pitchers can be as effective as they are perplexing, and listed Phil Niekro and Charlie Hough as the best he had seen. He further said he didn't really like to face that particular pitch. He believed that the knuckleball was so difficult to hit simply because "it's something different, something you don't see too much. It kind of messes [up] your swing a little."

Galarraga said his way of adjusting to a knuckleballer was "to stay back and see the ball and try to finally hit it somewhere. It's not easy." In fact, it's so difficult, Charlie Lau commented, "There are two theories on hitting the knuckleball. Unfortunately, neither of them works."

Roberto Alomar disagreed. He said going up against a knuckler doesn't always upset a batter's swing and timing. "It depends," he said. "Sometimes. Before, I didn't hit them; now I'm hitting them pretty good. I think you have to stay back on the ball. Just try to hit the ball through the middle. And hopefully, they hang it."

One theory is that big swingers, the power hitters, are less effective against the knuckleballers than slap hitters. However, Alomar said, "I think a big guy, if he can stay back on the ball good, like Canseco, he has a chance to hit good. I think the key is hopefully [the pitcher] will get behind in the count and have to throw you a fastball. If the knuckleball is 'knuckling' real good, it's going to be hard to hit."

In 2002 Bill Selby said, "I faced [Steve] Sparks the other day. The one thing about [knuckleballers] is you know you're going to get a knuckleball, so it's not a big secret. [But] it's [the ball's path] unpredictable. One might drop one way; one might stay up in the zone, or whatever. So, as far as change, I don't really change anything other than try to just play pepper and quit trying to drive the ball so much. You have to just stand out there and play pepper and use your hands more."

When told that Gwynn said he didn't change his approach against *any* type of pitcher other than knuckleball specialists, Selby suggested Gwynn probably works on using his hands more also. He granted that wasn't too difficult for Gwynn, as "he's always used his hands so good anyway."

Bumbry, a former Oriole, explained that Cal Ripken Jr. might adjust his stance, while Gwynn didn't. "Ripken was the kind of guy that always tinkered and changed his stance based on how he was swinging the bat and how he felt and how the pitcher was pitching him. But guys like Tony Gwynn had pretty much a set stance and they stayed within that stance. Now, I'm sure Tony made some slight adjustments, whether it be mental or physical to what the pitcher was doing, but Tony Gwynn is the kind of guy that had great bat control. And bat control simply means you put the fat [part of the] bat on the ball more times than not and you hit the pitch where it's pitched.

"He wasn't a power-type guy, he was more of a line-drive type guy. Cal was more of a power type. So, Tony had his set pattern and his set way of doing things, and he didn't change very much, although he did make some minor adjustments. But nothing as dramatic as you see [with] the changes and different stances that Cal made through his career."

Incidentally, Gwynn was once asked if he would make more drastic accommodations if, instead of being in a routine spot during the season, he was in a key moment of, say, the deciding game of the World Series. Gwynn, never lacking confidence and possessing an analytical mind, said he'd have to weigh all the factors such as who was on the mound and how late it was in the game. Then, and only then, did he concede, "I might [change], but only till I got two strikes, then I'd go back to my normal approach."

Henderson said that throughout his career he made a slew of adjustments to pitchers and their offerings. "I try to do a lot of that. A guy might be throwing a hard slider, a hard breaking ball, and I can't get it—I just try to hit the ball right out of the catcher's glove. I got fooled on some breaking balls that the catcher just knew he was about to catch it, then [I hit it] right out of his glove, and he wonders, 'How did you hit that ball?' I just say, 'I'm just trying to save me another pitch.' I just flick it, dead at it."

He said such adjustments come during an at-bat and during a given game, "especially if they're getting you out on something, so you try to adjust to get the advantage for you."

Cy Young Award winner Rick Sutcliffe felt that the great hitters are able to make adjustments. He said that in order for a player to make changes from, for example, at-bat to at-bat, or even from one trip into a city until the next to face a given pitcher, "you have to have a good memory."

While Merv Rettenmund agrees that adapting is important, one thing he doesn't teach his hitters is moving in the box to adjust for a pitcher's specific pitch, such as a sinkerball. Some hitters will move up in the box in an effort to get that pitch before it dips, but Rettenmund argues, "If you want to beat a sinkerball pitcher, why not move back and don't swing? Make him throw the ball all the way to the bat."

Vizquel said that he always factors in the pitcher he is facing on a given day. "You have to play the situations. Sometimes you got a pitcher that you think that you can pull, [so] maybe you get closer to the plate, where maybe you get away from the plate on some other guys."

Therefore, even though Vizquel is certainly not a power hitter, at times he will try to jack the ball, perhaps pulling it with just enough oomph to carry down the line for a homer. His home-run output has ranged from zero several seasons early in his pro career to a rather unexpected 14 in 2002. "I think hitting is an adjustment process. Every pitcher is different; you have to approach him different. I think that's when you start picking up [on that]—when you're a veteran player."

With experience, hitters begin to see more out there on the diamond. According to hitting instructor Charlie Manuel, smart hitters will "try to find signs, like seeing infielders that move, or outfielders or catchers that move in or out [prior to a pitch]. If you study the game, you can pick up a whole lot." Further, once a player picks up some information, he then has to adjust to and make use of it, taking what the defense is showing and giving him.

Another change young players must get used to is playing a very long season at the major-league level. Playing day in and day out for 162 games is grueling. Many fans wonder what wears a player out more, the physical aspects of the game or the mental. One could easily argue for the mental part. Concentrating on every single pitch and analyzing what may come next isn't easy.

As Travis Fryman said, "That's the challenge of baseball—the day-in, day-out ability to mentally prepare yourself to play. It's the hardest skill to learn in major-league baseball. That's why it takes young players several years before they become a consistent player. Richie Sexson was dealing with that earlier this year [2000]. It's a learning process; it takes time and patience on the part of an organization, the individual, and fans as well."

As good as Fryman was, even he had to pay some dues. He felt he played with intensity from his rookie year on. However, he stated, "What takes time is to learn how to have that constant approach, how to put the ups and downs behind you, and not ride your emotions so much as a young player or any young person does. They're very controlled by their emotions. As an old player, you learn how to even those things out a little bit."

Robby Thompson also recalled when he was young and left the minors, ready to become a big leaguer. Certain insight and lessons came with the territory. "First of all," he said, "it's a game of adjustments. [When] you get up here, pitchers are trying to figure you out. You're a rookie player, new kid on the block, so to speak. You may get that pitcher for awhile, but veteran pitchers are going to make adjustments. Then it's up to the player, the young kid, to make adjustments at the plate. That's probably the biggest thing that guys need to realize once they come up here: you just can't stay with that same approach and game plan time and time again. You have to make good judgments along with the pitcher."

When Willie Harris made the jump from Triple-A ball to the majors in August 2002, Thompson said such a transition was a tough one because pitchers "don't miss too many spots up here. You've got to be ready to hit on any count."

Likewise, when Cleveland's Jody Gerut came into the majors, he was astounded at how good pitchers such as Billy Koch were. "I never faced a guy throwing a 90-mph slider," Gerut said respectfully. "You don't run into them in the minors because they don't stay there long."

Young hitters must also learn to adjust very quickly once they enter the world of pro baseball. The transition from high school baseball to playing ball in the minors is as sudden as it is cruel. When Sexson was eighteen years old, he was a couple of weeks out of high school, playing ball for the Indians at their Burlington, North Carolina, farm team. His reaction: "This is a long way from home. I've never been to North Carolina before. I went to New York once. But that was with my parents.

"I can't believe the pitching here. In high school I never saw anything but a fastball. Here guys throw curveballs. Even with 3-0 counts. They change speeds. This is really something. In high school I was hitting around .470. I'd settle for half that right now." He was hitting .185 when he spoke those words back in 1993.

His story is typical. For many minor-league players, their first year in pro ball is also the first time they struggle mightily at the plate. For them, the minor leagues become a Darwinian world where truly only the strong survive and only those who are fit to play the game enjoy survival.

Then there are those who smoothly move up to the majors only to become baseball's version of singers who are known as one-hit wonders. These are the hitters who display a great deal of potential early in their career, then never pan out. One example of a player with such a meteoric career is Pat Listach, who won the Rookie of the Year Award over Kenny Lofton; he played only 215 games in the majors after his initial season.

Bagwell theorized, "A part of it is injuries; the other part is when the league makes adjustments to you. So you have to make adjustments to the league. The people who can't do it—they don't continue to be at that same level."

Haselman said that for rookies and veterans alike, when it comes to making changes, be it with bat selection, stance, or any nuance, players are doing it all the time. "[If] you're not feeling right at the plate, maybe you change your stance a little bit or your hand positioning. Maybe you get a lighter bat, maybe you get a heavier bat. It can be all kinds of different things. It's just a matter of how you feel. If you're feeling good, you don't change anything."

Along those lines, Arizona's Junior Spivey devoted a great deal of time working on a much-needed alteration to his swing back in 1998, and did so by playing fall ball. It was then that he learned to turn on the ball. "Good fastballs inside were tying me up, and I had to adjust." He said that fall ball in Arizona was perfect for him because he "needed more experience, more at-bats, more pitches [to see and deal with], and [more and different types of] pitchers."

Clearly there's a lot to learn. So much, in fact, that it wasn't until 2002 that Sammy Sosa said he finally felt he was at the top of his game, because he had made the adjustments necessary to stay on top. It was as if he let out a sigh; finally, he was no longer a free swinger but had become a man with a plan.

A few years ago Klesko spoke of another evolution he underwent as a hitter. "I worked harder, smarter; I know my zone. I'm not swinging at as many bad pitches. I'm not striking out but maybe half—a little more than half—of what I used to. So, obviously, when you're putting the ball in play more and you're hitting the ball solidly more [often], and you're drawing your walks more, you're going to hit better for a higher average."

While most experts stress the importance of making contact, there are exceptions. Thome is an unusual hitter in that while he strikes out often, he can hit for a decent average, he hits for power, and he draws tons of walks too—a rarity, especially nowadays. He admits he has a hole in his game. "My flaw is I swing and miss," he told *Baseball Digest*. "If I struck out as much as I do and never walked, I'd be concerned. Walks help your team win. One hundred walks are like 100 hits." So, in a way, his adjustment to striking out is, rather contradictorily, to develop an eye that enables him to coax many walks.

7

On Slumps and Streaks

THERE'S AN OLD story, probably apocryphal, about how one should respect a hot streak. Back in 1941 two friends were remarking on Joe DiMaggio's hitting streak, which had reached 20 games or so. One said that as good as DiMaggio was, his luck was bound to run out; the other contended that a smart bettor rides a streak and challenged his friend to a wager.

They agreed to bet $5 on whether DiMaggio would extend the streak or go hitless that day. When DiMaggio hit safely that day, the loser of the bet said he'd go with the same bet the next day. On and on went the streak, and on and on went the stubborn bettor. Late in the streak, it is said, he even increased his bet some nights, saying, "He just *can't* keep this up forever." Well, by the time he finally won the bet—before he could say, "I told you so," he was down a large chunk of money. The scenario is reminiscent of the old Damon Runyon quote: "It may be that the race is not always to the swift, nor the battle to the strong—but that is the way to bet."

Then again, a player can be cruising along nicely, then suddenly go cold—like a pitcher such as Steve Blass or, more recently, Mark Wohlers

and Rick Ankiel, who mysteriously lost their taken-for-granted, fundamental ability to throw strikes. While most players and coaches can't really
explain streaks and slumps, they know one when they experience it.

Ryan Klesko said that when he's in the midst of a scorching hitting
streak, he can actually attribute his success to several factors. "Obviously
you're seeing the ball well, you're more in a zone, a hitter's zone. Basically
you're getting a good pitch to hit for the most part, and you're feeling confident enough that you can handle that pitch so you're not missing it. Your
timing is definitely on—your rhythm and your timing—but you're also in
your zone [in that] you're not swinging at bad pitches. It's kind of a combination of everything."

With baseball's sophisticated intelligence system in place now, why
don't pitchers avoid a hitter when they know he's on a tear? Klesko said
that in part it's because the pitchers can't entirely avoid making a mistake
pitch or at least a pitch that, to a hot hitter, is tantalizing enough. "That's
being patient—aggressive, but patient in certain situations.

"If they throw that first-pitch fastball over the plate, you hit it hard.
If not, you wait and you understand that, for the most part, they have to
throw three strikes and most of the time they're going to make a mistake.
If you swing at a pitcher's pitch early in the count, you're going to get yourself out for the most part. And a lot of guys—most of the guys who hit
.300—they sit on a good pitch to hit. They can't handle all the pitches.
You've got guys like Vladimir Guerrero who can handle [pitches] up, in,
down, and away, but for the most part, most hitters have their strengths,
and if you sit on your strengths and be patient, that's when you're going
to be successful."

Still, Klesko recognized that, whether backed by scientific evidence
or merely by a gut feeling, it seems as if hot hitters get even more than
their fair share of lucky hits. "You're going to have your times when you
go 3 for 4 and don't even hit the ball good, but for the most part, when
you're in those streaks—you're hitting .400 for the month—you do have
some hits fall in and your line drives aren't getting caught. But you're making solid contact at least two or three times a game."

When a hitter makes that kind of contact that often, he will obviously earn more than his share of hits. That's especially true when one
considers that, during a typical game, hitters are lucky to get many good

pitches to hack at. Announcers like to say a hitter may get one really good pitch per at-bat, and he surely doesn't want to miss it, foul it off, or hit it poorly for a wasted at-bat. Klesko said that, naturally, the amount of tempting pitches he sees actually varies. "Sometimes you may get one or two a game, and sometimes you may get a lot more than that. And sometimes you just have to tip your hat to the pitcher on making good pitches. Other times you may have four or five pitches, and you foul them straight back. That's tough to do and still be successful."

The tip here is simple: be patient, wait for a good pitch, and when one comes, don't waste it—hit it with authority. "When you're hot," he pointed out, "you just don't miss them. You're making solid contact all the time."

Some announcers tell their audience that when a hitter smashes a foul ball that travels directly behind the plate into the net, it means the hitter was on the ball, but his bat just missed, by a scant margin, hitting the ball at the point and the angle where the ball would have soared in the other direction, into center field for a solid hit.

Klesko doesn't entirely agree. "I don't know. If you're fouling a lot of pitches straight back, especially two, three, four days in a row, I don't think you're right on it—you're missing the ball. I mean, you're getting a piece of it, but something is wrong.

"Just fouling it straight back," he continued, "is actually not even making as much solid contact as a high fly ball to center. You actually hit more of the ball [when it goes into play to center]. But a lot of guys when they foul it straight back—yeah, you may be right on it to a point where the bat head is right in the middle of the zone of the ball, but you may be under it. You just basically have to make the adjustment [and realize] 'Hey, I'm swinging under the ball; I better hit more of the middle of the ball.'

"Sometimes a pitcher's ball angles down a little bit. A lot of [pitchers] that get a lot of strikeouts—their ball has that straightness to it, to where you get a lot of guys who pop up or swing underneath it. Guys like [Curt] Schilling—their ball stays on that same plane, and other guys throw downhill more. So it's just a game of adjustments. You have to see what the pitcher's doing. [Against] some guys, you try to hit on top of the ball, and [against other] guys [whose pitches are sinking], you got to hit through the ball." Those who achieve this will have more streaks than slumps.

As fine a hitter as Joe Torre was, he never had as torrid a stretch as he enjoyed during his 1971 explosion. He said, "I hit the ball hard pretty much all year. I was very locked in mentally: that was the big thing. Focus-wise, concentration-wise, it was a heckuva year." That's pretty safe to say of a year in which he topped the NL with his lusty .363 average while also leading the league in hits (230), runs driven in (137), and total bases (352).

Torre said he benefited in that everything from bloopers to broken bats resulted in hits. "You need your share of those babies," he smiled, "[because] some line drives are going to be caught." Actually, he didn't get every break. Never a fleet runner, Torre remembered with a chuckle, "I was as light as I ever was the year I won the crown [at 205 pounds], but winning the crown had nothing to do with my speed, I'll guarantee you that.

"But it was one of those years: I don't think I ever went two games without a base hit, and I don't think that happened after July. It was crazy. It was just one of those freak years. It was just a very confident year, and I knew what I was going to hit off pitchers every day. You knew you were going to hit the slider off this guy, or he's going to give me the fastball to hit. It was really one of those unusual years, and I just made the most of it."

He again touched upon his locked-in concentration during his year-long streak. He compared the feeling to "being in a dark room. No disturbances whatsoever. I hit .363 against right-handers and .362 against left-handers, something weird like that. And every month I hit about the same number of home runs, same number of RBIs. It was a year that I was very proud of."

In a *Baseball Digest* article John Kruk likened a hitting tear to "an out-of-body experience." When he enjoyed a 19-game hitting streak, he said, "I just felt it didn't matter what they threw in there. You just see everything."

Hitters say that when they're not hitting well, they feel as if the pitch gets on them in a hurry, that they have no time at all to respond to the pitch. Even when things are going well, a major-league hitter has only a microsecond to pick up the ball, recognize its spin, determine its path and where it will end up, and decide whether or not he should swing. And that's simplifying things. He also has to have considered if he should be aggressive or not depending upon factors such as the count, the pitcher he's facing, the game situation, and bits of data such as what park he's in and the weather conditions.

Keith Hernandez, the 1979 National League MVP, said that when he was in the groove, it felt like he had three or four seconds to make all his decisions. Other hitters have said that when they're hitting well, the ball looks as big as a grapefruit, as opposed to the pea-size appearance of the ball when they are struggling.

Most experts also agree that home runs often come in bunches, subscribing to the country-and-western–inspired "when you're hot, you're hot; when you're not, you're not" theory of slugging. To further illustrate that contrast, Rod Carew once observed, "When I'm hitting [well], the ball comes up to the plate like a basketball. You can see the stitches and the writing on the ball. When you're not hitting, you don't see anything."

Some players see slumps as the reverse side of a hitting-streak coin. Klesko commented, "A lot of times you're missing balls, you're missing pitches you should hit hard. Also, you got a little bad luck—guys are making good plays on you. When it gets to that part, it gets mental. You come to the park, you've got to keep your head up. The younger kids—you try to tell them, 'Hey, hang in there. It's a new day. You may get four hits today.' If you go up to the plate thinking you're in a slump or you don't have that confidence, it's tougher to get a hit."

Bobby Murcer had an interesting take on slumps. "You decide you'll wait for your pitch. Then as the ball starts toward the plate, you think about your stance. And then you think about your swing. And then you realize that the ball that went past you for a strike was your pitch."

Texas hitting coach Rudy Jaramillo said that hitters know when things aren't right. They also realize that even when things are off—even just a bit—they can swoon into a full-fledged slump. He empathized, "You get lost in that rhythm, the timing with the pitcher. It's something real small all the time that gets you off, and that's, as a coach, what you have to figure out so these guys don't stay in a prolonged slump. You got to try to cut it off when you see it, not let it go three or four days and say, 'Well, let's see if he's going to adjust,' because you're losing at-bats."

Jaramillo said that the old theory of letting a hitter work his way out of a slump is nonsensical. "You can't do that. You got to start building that confidence back in him through drills and early work and whatever it takes."

McCraw is also a detractor of the "hit your way out of it" approach because "you might go through another ten games without getting a base hit, but you might get a bunt and come out of it the next game."

Johnny Damon lamented, "When I go into slumps, I hit a lot of lazy fly balls. Lazy fly balls aren't going to fall in too much, but if you keep the ball on the ground, make the defense work, you also have a chance to get [the ball] through the infield." He added that a rare player like Ichiro Suzuki can usually avoid slumps. "He's what every team wants right now: a guy who can keep it in play. He's just a great handler of the bat."

As a rule, Klesko feels it's easier for a veteran to shake out of a slump than an inexperienced player. "You accept it. You know you're going to go through your slumps. Then you [also] have your ways of getting out of it— you know yourself and your swing as a veteran." It's reminiscent of what former catcher Terry Kennedy once said: "Most slumps are like the common cold. They last two weeks no matter what you do."

Klesko continued, "Plus, you don't let guys mess with you. When you're younger, everybody on the team is trying to help you out. If I get in [a slump], there aren't too many guys [who are] going to come up and talk to me unless they know my swing."

It is typical, as Klesko was indicating, for a young hitter to be almost in awe of older players, assuming they know more and can tell anyone how to snap out of a slump. However, if a youngster listens to too many voices, that can mess him up, too. With age comes the realization that a player knows his own swing best, knows not to panic, and perhaps even has the ability to come out of slumps on his own.

When Thome was mired in a slump in 2000, he was wise enough to remain philosophical. He told an Indians announcer, "Look, I know I'm going to have my good times; I know I'm going to have my bad times. I've just got to try to maintain the same approach and realize that eventually I will come out of it."

Sometimes it really does help to have a positive attitude about a slump, perhaps even laugh it off. Once when he was with Philadelphia in 1999, Scott Rolen was in the midst of a tough time, punctuated by a game in which he whiffed five times. After that ordeal, he joked, "I've always prided myself on never striking out four times in a game—and I still haven't."

However, even a veteran can become frustrated. In the early 1990s Kent Hrbek was in the throes of an August slump. After finally enjoying his first three-RBI day since June 10, he joked, "I'm just trying stance #558. It worked a couple of times." Actually, though, most experts think such drastic change is self-defeating. Hrbek could have been guilty of a crime many slumping hitters commit: trying, thinking, and changing too much. It's human nature to do so when floundering, but, again, it may be an unwise thing to do. While most players realize slumps are inevitable, they still struggle.

Florida's Mike Lowell suffered through a long dry spell during the second half of the 2002 season. Everything seemed to go against him. For example, in August he fouled a ball into the stands, but Jeff Kent raced over and plucked the ball as he dove into a row of fans. Lowell complained, "We have five fans that don't know how to catch the ball." Had they provided him with a home-field advantage, he would have had another swing. Of course, bogged down in a slump, he may well have merely popped the ball up again.

That same month, Andres Galarraga's hitting was off. His manager, Frank Robinson, benched him for a day. Robinson stated, "We're going to see if he can correct a couple of mechanical things he does wrong at the plate. He's out of whack because he's too quick with the body. When [the pitch] is away, he hits it with the end of the bat because he's reaching, and that results in soft fly balls or ground balls. When it's inside, if he swings, he's going to get jammed." Robinson said that he wanted Galarraga to remedy the situation by slowing his body down and by shortening up on his stride.

Some hitters try to snap themselves out of a slump by making extra trips to the batting cage. Some do the opposite: they go out on the town, avoid talking or thinking about baseball, and hope the next day the slump vanishes.

Announcer Matt Underwood said he once heard an unusual bit of advice about coming out of a slump. Matt Williams told him that when he was struggling he had to work hard at trying easier. He felt that if he pressed and got tense, he was lost. He had to change his frame of mind, forcing himself to relax, even while in the midst of anguish. "I think that's right on the money," said Underwood. "It's what guys should do, but it's very difficult for some guys to do. Some guys continue to press and get more frustrated."

Long ago, when Hornsby was asked how he worked himself out of a slump, he replied, "By trying to hit the ball back at the pitcher. In fact, I always tried to hit the ball back through the box, because that is the largest unprotected area."

Sometimes slumps begin due to the park one is hitting in. Fenway Park, wrote Bernardo Leonard in *The Superstar Hitter's Bible*, is known to be a "slump-starter for right-handed hitters." He added that hitting in a locale such as Wrigley Field on a cold day is tough, especially when trying to hit a pitch when it's in on the raw, numb hands. Because of that, "you may not be able to execute the proper swing for the rest of the day." When that happens, a hitter may change his normal swing, get in bad habits, and experience the birth of a slump.

Playing on a day with the wind blowing in can do the same, as, according to Bernardo, "batters tend to overswing to compensate. You overswing and failure usually follows. Likewise, when the wind is blowing out, you try to loft the ball into the jet stream." To do so is, once more, changing a normal swing, which can only lead to problems.

In other instances, though, the reason a batter slumps against a certain pitcher is clear: The pitcher is simply good, capable of putting any hitter into a funk. Galarraga said that over the years one man has always seemed to have his number: "Schilling. Why? Because he's got great control; he throws the ball where he wants it. He throws hard with good speed. [He has a] good slider, good sinker. I mean it's really tough to track him — he throws in different locations all the time."

Another theory is that a slumping player should try to bunt for a cheap hit. The thinking here is that once the dam of the slump breaks with a hit, the flow of pent-up hits will surge. Such logic may work, or it may merely be an example of superstitious thinking. Either way, a number of players do subscribe to such ideas.

Still, McCraw said that the reason why a bunt just might snap a cold spell for some hitters is a logical one. "If you're going to bunt the ball, you're going to have to watch it. You have to keep your head on it, your eyes on it." Still, while he dislikes the hitting-out-of-a-slump approach, he conceded that "everybody's got their own philosophy. I've seen Frank Robinson lay down a bunt, and he's in the Hall of Fame."

As devastating as a prolonged slump can be, Whitey Herzog knew that good hitters bounce back. If one of his players, even an older one, languished through an entire off-season, instead of panicking and trying to dump the player, Herzog assumed the poor showing was an aberration. Such patience benefited his team, with hitters often flourishing under him, owing him loyalty, and paying off with big offensive numbers.

8

Hitters' Attitudes

TY COBB CONSIDERED hitters to be baseball's heavy artillery. If that's so, then he must have been a Sherman tank, instilling fear in pitchers. As he phrased it, "Every great hitter works on the theory that the pitcher is more afraid of him than he is of the pitchers." He was so driven to win, Branch Rickey observed, "Cobb lived off the field as though he wished to live forever. He lived on the field as if he thought it was his last day." Cobb even said once that he'd "kill anyone that gets in my way."

Mike Schmidt stressed the importance of the first confrontation between hitter and pitcher. "If I hit the fastball hard, it tells me I can handle his velocity that night. It also gives the pitcher the same thought."

In his prime, third baseman Vinny Castilla also exuded a quiet confidence, knowing that he had a bat so quick nobody blew a fastball by him. Even the blazing fastballer Billy Wagner said, "Vinny loves hitting against me. Power. He's straight power, a straight bomber."

There is little argument about how important it is to be confident and ambitious. Stories abound about how Cobb was so good because he was so driven, to the point of being obsessive about his game. Some say he was somehow trying to prove to his deceased father just how good he was. Others say Cobb never gave away an at-bat. If he was 3 for 3 late in the game, he wasn't satisfied; he wanted to go 4 for 4.

Cal Ripken Jr. was a boy who, according to his father in his book, *The Ripken Way*, always "had a very competitive nature. He always wanted to win at all costs, no matter what the game was." In board games, Cal Jr. would even swipe $500 bills from the bank if the other players were distracted. Although he didn't have the psychological baggage that Cobb toted, he had Cobb-like intensity.

Rickey Henderson believed that Reggie Jackson's secret to success was that "he always wanted to be in the limelight, he always wanted to be the money man. When the game was on the line, he always wanted to be the guy to take over." So, just as an Albert Belle was fueled by hatred at times, Jackson's ego propelled him. "He's the [guy] I liked to see in clutch situations," said Henderson.

Another former Yankee, Joe DiMaggio, had a reason to be confident; he was *good*. He not only hit for a high average, at .325 lifetime, he also hit for power (361 homers). What makes that even more impressive is that he struck out only 369 times in 1,736 major-league contests.

When Torre led the league in hitting, his confidence was a big part of his superb play. He asserted that, like Cobb, he was "never satisfied with two hits in a game. There were a lot of games where I got a hit the first time up, and that made it a little easier. Most of my hits like that were doubles to right center field. I just tried to think 'through-the-middle' all the time."

Young hitters need to think positively in order to make the leap from the minors to the major leagues. Selby, a Mississippi native who has spent quite a bit of time languishing at the minor-league level, spoke of such intangibles in 2000 when he had been called up to the Indians: "What goes through a baseball player's mind is the pressure, especially when you come to a [contending] team like this. You're out there everyday; you've got to do your job because it's important to win. At the minor-league level, a lot of times it's 'develop, get better, and get your at-bats.' Here it's 'help the team; you gotta win.' So that's the biggest difference."

To help players concentrate on a winning attitude and nothing else, Selby said that in the majors "everything is taken care of for you—the spreads [of fine food], the travel—everything's a lot easier; this is the pinnacle of baseball. But that's what you work for." It's also the reason why players can, paradoxically, relax more, yet worry more until they feel they belong.

After all, as Selby said, the attitude of the parent club is "If we called you up, that means you're good enough to play." Just as there is, according to a Tom Hanks film character, no crying in baseball, there is no holding of hands, either. Selby conceded that the major-league team's attitude is "You're here. Do what you can do and help us out when you're called on. Be ready."

Damon attributes some of his success to playing baseball "at an early age, and I was able to get on the playgrounds and hone my skills. When you build that confidence that you're one of the better players around— you definitely need confidence when you play in the big leagues because it can easily be taken away from you." Knowing that he is talented, and realizing that baseball can be a humbling game, Damon simply tries to "go out there and have fun. I think that's what makes me the player that I am today."

Cal Ripken Sr. once wrote of the importance of confidence for hitters. He stated, "Anyone who watched Reggie [Jackson] play could see that he had a tremendous amount of self-confidence, and confidence is the key to any area of the game. You have to have confidence to hit."

Jerry Kindall, a renowned college coach at the University of Arizona, authored the book *Science of Coaching Baseball*. He pointed out that when a player has confidence he will tend to play well and he will, therefore, feel good about himself and his skills. That feeling of buoyant self-esteem can lead to even more success. As Kindall phrased it, a player who is confident "trusts his ability, has control of himself, has all positive images in his head, is thinking all positive thoughts, is relaxed, is paying attention to what he needs to be, and is mentally prepared to play." However, Kindall knew that for most hitters "confidence is as hard to hang on to as a good knuckleball." A hitter like Jackson is able, by and large, to hang on to his blend of cockiness, seemingly suffering from few self-doubts.

Early on, Omar Vizquel didn't possess much of a stick. On the playground he could almost have been saddled with the ignominious label "automatic out." He admitted that he did have doubts about his hitting ability. "Yes," he began, "you question yourself when you're hitting and not when you're fielding. Because you've been playing baseball for a long time, people [say], 'When you are good at something, why not be good at another one? Don't doubt yourself; just go get them.' But it [the doubt] does happen."

Rolen was extremely unhappy in Philadelphia in 2001 and into 2002, playing under the fiery Bowa. They clashed, and Rolen's statistics did not reflect his ability. When the Phils finally swapped him, Rolen was warmly accepted in St. Louis and he thrived there.

If a player perceives that there is a problem with the front office, his manager, or something else, then there *is* a problem. If a hitter begins to sulk or feud with his manager, there's a good likelihood his hitting will suffer. The same often occurs when trade talks about a player begin to swirl or when there's a contract dispute or renegotiation talk. That's why players often demand that their team either signs them to a contract before the season begins or waits until season's end—they want no distractions whatsoever during the season.

In sports and in other arenas, there is an interesting concept known as the self-fulfilling prophecy. This basically states that if a person believes something is going to happen, then it will. An example is a young basketball player at the free throw line in a clutch situation. If he thinks, "I can't make this shot," then he probably won't.

This psychological phenomenon may partially explain why, once a hitter discovers he has a hard time hitting a certain pitcher, his woes continue. Babe Ruth seemingly crushed just about every pitcher he ever faced. However, Hub Pruett, an obscure pitcher, for some mysterious reason crushed Ruth's spirit, striking him out exactly half the times he faced the Bambino. The situation probably got to the point where Ruth believed that he could not hit this guy, and he didn't.

Perhaps the ultimate example of how players' collective confidence (or lack of it) can influence team performance came in the 1927 World Series. Baseball lore has it that in batting practice before the first game of the clash between the Murderer's Row Yankees and the Pirates, an army of New York hitters pounded ball after ball out of Forbes Field. Watching in awe were the Pittsburgh hitters, solid players, but hardly leviathan sluggers. Legend says that after observing this display of power, the Pirates were mentally defeated, doomed to lose, while the muscle-flexing Yanks felt good and confident. The result was a four-game sweep for the Yankees of Ruth, Lou Gehrig, and company.

The Yankees' onslaught was much like the times when a feeling of euphoria permeates an entire lineup and good hitting becomes contagious. One example is baseball's slugfests. Such a game starts innocently, but before you know it, the game is out of hand as a parade of hitters lashes out hit after hit. Inexplicably, aside from the confidence factor, the hitters rip the ball regardless of who comes out of the opposing team's bullpen.

It's as if one hitter thinks, "If the other guys can hit him, so can I." The following batters must be thinking alike, and the self-fulfilling prophecy once again comes into play. A look at a typical box score from such games usually yields stats such as everyone in the lineup either scored a run or drove in a run, and everyone but, say, the number nine batter had at least one hit.

Hitters consider it a joy when they step into the box to face a pitcher who seemingly can't get them out. They own that pitcher—and they wear him out. It's as if they know what the pitcher is going to throw, and that knowledge gives hitters confidence and a decided edge. It's a strange situation; call it an inexplicable jinx over a given pitcher. In baseball's early days such a pitcher was called the batter's "cousin." And it even happens regardless of the hitter's lifetime stats.

Why does this happen? Merv Rettenmund, who has studied the art of hitting as much as anyone, replied succinctly and honestly, "I can't answer that. I've watched it for years. I mean, you'll watch a guy walk onto the mound and throw a no-hitter against the best-hitting club in baseball, but some guy at the end of the order is hitting .750 off of him.

"The catcher [Mike] Redmond in Florida—he's the number two or three-string catcher for the Marlins; off of Tom Glavine it's like he's got a 1.000 [batting average]. You can't get him out, but they're trying to pitch to him. One day at a [Braves team] meeting I asked, 'Why pitch to him? It's not working. Don't pitch to him or just throw it right down the middle—keep throwing him fastballs there. It's impossible for him to raise his batting average. That's why the game is what it is. After all the years I've been in it, I'm looking for answers every day and there are none."

Dr. Maher knows the importance of the psychology of the sport. He agreed with Sam McDowell, who believes that in spite of wealth and apparent success, most players lack self-esteem. Maher said, "I divide the self into two areas: Self One and Self Two. Self One has to do with the ego; it has to do with what you think about yourself in relation to other people. That's where the problem is. It's very critical: you put pressure on yourself, you lose your self-esteem when you don't perform well.

"Self Two is the performer. They just let it happen; you go out and play the game. Some major-league players have difficulty with their self and their self-esteem—it can come and go." Most players, even with some trouble in this area, still achieve due to sheer talent, but some have been done in by self-esteem issues.

In short, if a kid comes along and has the physical skills and the raw talent to play the game, as long as his self-esteem holds out, he will last for a long time in the majors. "He will be resilient," began the doctor. "He'll bounce back. If he gets injured or has a poor string of at-bats or whatever, he will come back. He'll enjoy playing the game."

Travis Fryman said that fear is a definite mental factor for hitters; however, it isn't a fear of failure but rather a "fear of embarrassment. I don't think failure is anything to be afraid of. I think you prepare to succeed, you expect to perform well, but what's the fear of failing in baseball? A little bit of embarrassment. You're not going to be physically hurt if you fail, so I don't think you need to be afraid to fail, but I think you should be afraid not to prepare to succeed. There's a difference there."

Sometimes a young player doesn't do well if at first he feels a bit out of place or unfamiliar with his new environment. Richie Sexson explained, "You obviously have to go through a transitional stage from high school [moving up to pro ball] more so than a guy that's in college [then advances]. When you're in high school, you don't really get to play a whole bunch of night games. Wooden bats are something new. Nine-inning games are strange for some people, as they were for me. And it's tough, for the first time, to move away from your family. It's hard to do."

Likewise, when some players are traded for the first time, their confidence level takes a hit. Tyler Houston, when he was with Milwaukee, said that shouldn't be the case. "There might be insecurity when you first get there [to a new team] because you don't know anybody. It's like being the new kid in school: you kind of sit there and be quiet until spoken to and try to blend in as well as possible." He said that players shouldn't have the attitude that they were cast off, unwanted. "You got to look at it like, 'This team wanted me.'" He said that was especially true because players realize trades are simply part of the game.

When a hitter is thrown at, it can lead to a strange mixture of emotions. Batters sometimes grudgingly say that they have a tacit respect for pitchers who aren't afraid to come in tight to them. Of course, they'd prefer the pitcher didn't; for that matter, they'd prefer if an old rule of baseball was reinstated—the one that permitted the hitter to indicate to the pitcher where he wanted each pitch to be thrown!

Brent Butler, a second baseman for the 2002 Colorado Rockies, had an interesting point of view. "It kind of works both ways. I mean, as a hitter, you stand back in there [after being brushed back or hit by a pitch] and you let them know that you're not bothered by that. I think definitely it [the tight pitch] sends a message from a pitcher, but, again, if a hitter just gets back up and stands right back in there with no fear, then it kind of sends a message back."

Pitcher Paul Shuey said, "If somebody throws at my head, what happens is I get scared. And when you get scared, you have either [of] two reactions—either you get scared and you stay scared, or you get really, really pissed. And when I get really, really pissed, watch out, man. I'm coming at you; I'm coming at anybody." He said it's a matter of instinct. "You either get angry and try to get even, or you're going to be kinda' scared and try to get out, and that's not the way to go about this game out here." You can't play well in fear.

So, add the quality of near-fearlessness to the list of big-league hitting secrets. Be aware too that no hitter is entirely fearless; being afraid of a baseball thrown by a major-league pitcher is as normal as a newborn fearing loud noises or any sane adult fearing fire. And make no mistake, being hit by a fastball hurts. Being able to stand in the box while basically ignoring fear is a quality hitters must have, especially after coming back from being injured by a beanball.

In Ernie Harwell's *Tuned to Baseball,* he quotes Sparky Anderson as saying that the three men he felt were immune to pitchers' intimidation were Pete Rose, Lee May, and Chet Lemon. Anderson stated, "There are some players today who can't stand up to the rough, knock-'em-down pitching of 30 years ago. But these three could handle themselves in any baseball era. None of them has any fear at the plate."

Nearly a quarter-century ago, Dodgers great Steve Garvey vividly displayed his fearlessness, doing what hitters such as Hank Aaron had done so many times—getting revenge for brushback pitches. Remarkably, Garvey was knocked down six times in 1980 and came back with a hit on each of those occasions.

Similarly, in a game in August 2002, San Francisco's Benito Santiago didn't get mad, he got even. The Pirates had walked Barry Bonds intentionally three times in order to avoid him while getting to Santiago. The third time up, the proud Santiago responded with a grand slam. His manager, Dusty Baker, said he could relate to Santiago's frustration and ire. "I hit behind Hank Aaron a lot of years. Yeah, it bothers you. I don't care what your name is."

Like confidence, pride is another quality that can boost a player's performance. From 1959 through 1961, Stan Musial suffered through substandard seasons. Instead of calling it quits at the age of 41, he worked hard in the off-season and vowed to bow out only after putting up some Musial-like numbers. The next year he hit .330, almost exactly his career batting average.

Writing off a player is always a tough decision. On one hand, there's an old saying, "It's better to trade a player a year early rather than a year too late." Get rid of a hitter while he still seemingly has value and, even if he enjoys one or two good seasons after being dumped, overall the swap will usually pan out to be a good one. On the other hand, if a team is wrong about the player being over the hill, it can be a huge mistake. Frank Robinson, like Musial a man of intense pride, was sent packing from the Reds to the Orioles after the 1965 season. Cincinnati was convinced that, at 30, Robinson was washed up. The next year he won the Triple Crown and went on to hit loads of homers after the Reds gave up on him.

Some players can handle such pressure and gain confidence, lasting for years in the majors, while others quickly bow out after developing an attitude of self-doubt and defeat.

Rickey Henderson was the type of player who had few, if any, self-doubts. Yet he said that at times he has felt somewhat underappreciated. However, instead of dwelling on that as a negative, he said that he realizes that someday, maybe even 20 years from now, the baseball community will have to fully appreciate what he has done. He said his numbers should continue to stand as records because nowadays any talented players who could feasibly break his records simply won't stay around long enough to do so.

He regrets that players of today tend to play strictly for the money. These players, he says, will stick around for awhile, take the money and run, and fall short of Henderson's coveted records. He believes that players should have the attitude he did, playing baseball "for the love of the game."

Darin Erstad is a throwback, a man who doesn't seem to get caught up in all the glory of the game. He not only plays with a football mentality, he's been likened to another gritty former football standout. "The only guy I can compare him to that I played with is Kirk Gibson in 1988," said Angels batting coach Mickey Hatcher. "He's determined to do everything he can to help his team win, and he was the guy who did the most to keep us competitive."

Erstad's manager, Mike Scioscia, also praised his mental make-up: "A guy with his intensity and talent comes around once in a generation. You are not going to find a guy who does everything he does."

Gibson, a former college football standout, was undoubtedly a take-charge leader. Sparky Anderson once called him "the next Mickey Mantle," while teammates simply called him dynamic. "He was the ultimate team player," Anderson continued. "When he went 0 for 4 and we lost, he could bite off the head of a rattlesnake. When he went 0 for 4 and we won, he ran around the clubhouse like he had hit two grand slams and stole the mustard off somebody's hot dog."

Ellis Burks has always displayed a positive attitude about his play. Despite chronic knee problems, he has amassed over 2,000 hits and over 300 homers. He did this by taking it one game at a time. "I always say that if you set goals, you are limiting yourself." His main goal is to stay healthy, saying, "If I'm healthy, I'm going to perform." When he's not at full ability, he still says he'll fight all year long, trying "to dig and scratch to get some hits."

Managers appreciate such an attitude. Burks's Cleveland manager in 2003, Eric Wedge, commented, "The guy has two bad knees and runs hard to first base on every ground ball. If that's not leadership, what is?"

Cal Ripken Sr. wrote in *The Ripken Way*, "When Cal was young, he'd ride along in the car with me to the ballpark. On most every ride, we talked baseball: fundamentals, strategy, trends, techniques—basically we talked about anything that had to do with baseball." Cal Sr. said he had no idea how big an impact it made on his son. But through a form of baseball osmosis, all those talks paid off years later as Cal Jr. developed and maintained a great attitude toward baseball.

Cal Sr. believed that his son's work ethic and iron will came at least in part from both his parents. Senior was not the type of player to ask for a day off, and Junior also fought days off with the ardor of a crusader. Cal Sr. tried to impart the idea of staying on task and focused, resulting in a built-in edge over the opposition. He let his sons and players know that the cliché "It's not practice that makes perfect, it's perfect practice that makes perfect" is true even at the major-league level.

He was also wise enough to realize—and to pass on to others—that at least a part of perfect practice includes considering the mental side of baseball, not merely the physical side. According to Jerry Kindall in his book *Science of Coaching Baseball*, "Anywhere from 50 percent to 90 percent of sports performance is mental."

For example, hitters should never give up on their craft or become complacent. Those who plug away may be well rewarded. Ozzie Smith and Omar Vizquel have more in common than their uncommon ability to play shortstop. Both made themselves into much better hitters toward the end of their careers. In 2002, for instance, by the Indians' 156th game, Vizquel had established personal highs for homers (14) and runs batted in (72).

Burks explained that sometimes this phenomenon happens due to hitters "being more patient. The older you get, you become more patient, and that's not only in sports, it's in everything in life. You think more. Instead of using your talent all the time, you use your brain a little more.

The older you get, you use each and every little advantage you have." So, the combination of maturity, patience, intelligence, plus hard work can, and has, turned even below-average hitters into solid ones.

Bumbry stated, "I guess it's a maturation thing and that they, over years, have learned a lot from having played and faced different pitchers. That's why they made their adjustments, and that's how they were able to make those adjustments. They recognized the fact that [changes] had to be made. But it's maturing more than anything else." Further, Bumbry said that tenacious hitters such as Vizquel are living proof that it's never too late to learn and players can, indeed, come on strong even toward the middle to latter stages of their careers.

When approached to discuss hitting and his improvements, Vizquel joked, "You're asking the wrong man here." When prodded, reminded that he had truly turned himself into a solid hitter, he said, "It takes a lot of years and it takes experience," almost parroting Bumbry's words. Vizquel, who had also worked with weights later in his career, added, "When you do a thing all over again and all over again, and you practice it, I think that's what makes you a better hitter.

"Obviously, I'm a better defensive player, and the offense wasn't going to come by itself. Just being around guys that really are great hitters—like, early in my career, I started with the Seattle Mariners and I watched Alvin Davis hit and I watched guys like Harold Reynolds. Then I came to Cleveland and I watched guys like Albert Belle, Carlos Baerga, Eddie Murray, Dave Winfield. You really start picking up little things that can help you out, and I think that's what I did."

He recalled one of his earliest lessons: "Being in the big leagues and switch hitting is not easy. I [began] switch hitting kind of late in my career when I was already in Triple-A, so it took me a long time to figure out the pitching and then how to hit from both sides of the plate. So it was a hard process for me." After working on it diligently, once he got that skill down, it was a boon to the offensive side of his game.

Henderson calls players such as Smith and Vizquel "late bloomers," adding, "Sometimes they have to get adjusted, and it just takes time to get adjusted to what they want to do. Then, all of a sudden, it clicks and they become steady ballplayers." Conversely, many superstars clicked from day one. Henderson said he believed that he was always a great player due to his athleticism. "I think I was a football-mentality type of guy," he said. "That's why I stole bases and hit the dirt a lot. Nothing fazed me too much." He then added two other intangible traits: determination and the will to win.

Pitcher Frank Tanana saw those same traits in Eddie Murray: "Some people thrive on clutch situations, and it elevates their ability. Eddie seems to have that innate ability to perform at his peak when the game is on the line."

Murray confirmed that, saying, "I love being on the spot, with the game on the line; that's where I want to be." He also believed that the pitchers' fear of him gave him an edge in such crucial match-ups.

Henderson relished pressure, too. Of playing in postseason games, Henderson said, "I love to be in the spotlight when everyone's eyes are on me." When he exploded with an awesome showing in the 1989 League Championship Series, Tony LaRussa opined, "It's got to be the best play-off series any player ever had." Henderson evaluated his own showing by saying, "I'm one of the money players, one of the guys who wants to be there when it counts." Henderson followed that up by hitting .474 in the World Series.

Hitters, even the record setters, must eventually retire, and the decision to quit is a heart-wrenching one. Even when circumstances seem to dictate to a hitter that it's time to give up the game, some men refuse. In four years with Toronto, Cecil Fielder's high-water mark for homers was 14. He went to Japan when it seemed as if he wasn't good enough to continue making it in the majors. When he returned to the States in 1990, his bat went berserk: he hit 51 homers, then followed it up the next year with 44 to cop two consecutive home-run derbies.

Julio Franco, who won a batting crown in 1991, had his career officially pronounced dead by big-league front offices. He spent time in Japan, Mexico, and Korea, playing in venues such as Chiba Lotte and Samsung before he rebounded. He knew he was back when he landed a job with the Atlanta Braves in 2001. By then he was about 43 years old (the veracity of his birth certificate is a bit shaky). Still, he endured, never doubting his ability to play the game.

Nor did Jim Thome. He goes through periods in which he flounders, but his father taught him not to show his emotions, telling him, "When you're struggling, don't let people see you're struggling." Thome appreciated the fact that his hitting coach, Charlie Manuel, taught him "to show up to work early and want to be in the lineup everyday. A splendid attitude."

As Torre knows so well, players' mental outlooks are important, and many other players sparkled in that department. He said of Atlanta star Dale Murphy, "He has the perfect attitude: when he's on the field, baseball is number one." After a draining 1982 season when his Braves won the Western Division title, Murphy actually spent some time in the Instructional League. That prompted a teammate to tease, "Murphy's going to be the only player ever to win the MVP one year and the Comeback Player of the Year Award the next season."

Jeff Abbott, who played for a handful of big-league teams, also had a great outlook on baseball. He played the game with a feeling that came from advice given to him from his father. "What my dad used to tell us is—when you'd lose, say, a Little League game and everybody would be crying—'Don't get too upset, because in five minutes you guys are all going to forget about this and you're going to have a good game tomorrow.'

"That's the advice he gave me when I was growing up that's special to me. It made me never get too high or low about the game. He said, 'Just brush it off and there'll be better days tomorrow.'" As an adult, Abbott synthesized all those words into a succinct phrase, "Just take it one game at a time."

In the *Arizona Fall League 2002 Program*, a profile on Anaheim sparkplug David Eckstein revealed the then–27-year-old's wonderful attitude. The diminutive shortstop realized that those who had seen him on the field were aware that he didn't "have the best skills. I don't hit the ball especially hard," he said, "but I understand my game. I always play hard, and I play toward my strengths. Work hard and play hard—that's what I have to do to stay up here."

His manager, Scioscia, said it simply, "This guy is a baseball player. He's a winner, a guy who has had to earn everything he has."

In a 2000 interview, veteran pitcher Doug Henry said that of all the players in the game at that time, the one player he respected the most was Bagwell. Henry liked his attitude, "He's a class act. He goes about his business. He plays the game hard. He's somebody who just goes out and plays the game like it should be played."

An old story illustrates the drive and single-mindedness of Hank Aaron. During the 1958 World Series, as Aaron stepped into the batter's box, catcher Yogi Berra noticed Aaron was holding his bat with its trademark away from Aaron's view. Hitters felt that if they couldn't see the trademark, the bat was being held in such a way that it was vulnerable to breaking. So Berra instructed Aaron to turn the label so he could read it. Aaron replied, "I came up here to hit, not to read."

Henderson said that for a player to be a success, it had to begin with a harsh lesson. "One thing I think I learned in the game first was how to fail," he said. "If I accepted failure, then I was OK." Of course, that's easy to say for a man who seldom failed, but it is an interesting approach to the vagaries of the game.

He said that he doesn't even believe in squawking with official scorers in an effort to get them to change calls or to plant the idea to give him future close-scoring decision calls. The impression is that the elder Henderson wants very much to be known as a nice guy. Still, he grants that when the games begin, he does appear to be intense, with a game face that rivals that of any NFL lineman.

Often when one discusses attitude in sports, it's to highlight the positive. However, in Barry Bonds's situation, the case is much more complex. Unlike Henderson, who seems bent on changing any negative images of himself, Bonds just doesn't seem to care. The phrase "Barry's Barry" has been used quite often to succinctly describe his unique talent as well as his personality, including his moodiness and his poor relationships with his peers and the media. However, some people believe Bonds's disregard for other people's opinion is an asset. He has only to answer to his own high standards, they contend. Whatever the truth about that, Bonds can continue to "be Barry" as long as his stellar productivity holds out.

Cobb, like a wrestling villain, delighted in being in an adversarial role; he felt it helped make him become a great hitter. Other players refused to room with him, even when he was only 18 years old. Later he said with venom in his voice, "I hated them as much as they hated me." He said he was "grateful for what they did for me by driving me off by myself. The attitude of my teammates gave me an added incentive. I wanted to be a great ballplayer to show up my teammates."

Often the truth about a player's bad attitude won't surface until he fades or retires. While players such as Bumbry say they never wanted out of the lineup, there are those who would ask for numerous days off. Yogi Berra felt that Joe Pepitone never lived up to his potential because he "never really matured." He'd frequently say that he felt sick and "begged not to play." Said Berra of the former Yankee, "Honestly, I don't think he took his career seriously enough."

9

Mannerisms, Stances, and Swings

ALTHOUGH IN TODAY'S game not many players choke up on the bat, such a tactic is still recognized as a way to gain better bat control. Wee Willie Keeler did it; so did Rose. Cobb not only choked up, he split his hands on the bat, leaving about an inch gap between his top and bottom hands. At times the Georgia Peach would slide his hands together for more power on a given pitch. Amazingly, among active players the biggest name player to still choke up is not a slap hitter, but a slugger.

Hitting coach Duane Espy said, "Bonds obviously [chokes up], and Sosa's up above that knob. I think there's a lot more of it [than most fans suspect]. With us [the 2002 Padres] Ronnie Gant does it most of the time. I think it's becoming more prevalent because of Bonds and what he's doing, but, once again, I think it's a comfort thing. Some guys like it and some guys don't like it."

Espy continued, "As much as anything, it's where the bat feels comfortable to them. If he [Bonds] held it on the knob or half way up, he'd probably still do the same thing."

Bonds's 601st homer was vivid testimony to his strength. He not only hit it while choking up, but also on a swing in which his bat broke in two. As the ball soared toward the wall, Bonds was left holding about one-fourth to one-third of his bat.

Rusty Staub was another hitter who had power yet chose to choke up. However, the hitters who choke up now are typically players such as Tony Womack and a small handful of others.

Merv Rettenmund believes that 30 or 40 years ago choking up made sense. "In my opinion," he began, "and I'm not saying I'm right on this, years ago that's the way they did it, and they had to do it because they used to use bats like Jackie Robinson's. Those bats used to be big bottle bats about 36 inches long and 36 ounces. With two strikes, they were tough to control." However, he thinks that now choking up is not only an almost lost art, it's an unnecessary one.

It's easy for, say, a fan to pontificate that today's hitters fan too much because they don't choke up. Rettenmund says, however, such advice is "a statement that people make if they want to sound smart, like they know what they're talking about." According to him, relying on such a bromide sounds good, but isn't in touch with today's game.

"Some of the bats these guys are using today are 32 ounces and 33 to 34 inches long. If you choke up on them, you have no bat left; it's ridiculous. Tony Gwynn—I bet he wasn't swinging over 31 ounces of wood. You ask him to choke up, he should hit with a pool cue then. Choking up? It's silly—today the bats are customized [for each hitter]."

Some batters do the opposite of choking up. Mantle, who once hit a ball that might have traveled 600 feet had it not smacked into the facade at old Yankee Stadium, was one of the power hitters who liked to hold the bat with his bottom hand actually extending off the bat. His little finger on that hand rested under the bat, much like Willie Stargell's did. The leverage he got on his swings was impressive, and the distances on his home runs were just as mind-boggling.

So, even though amateurs are taught to choke up with two strikes, over the years many sluggers, and now even nonsluggers, adhered to Ralph Kiner's old advice about swinging from the bottom of the bat because that's where home runs come from. And home-run hitters, he pointed out, drive Cadillacs—or, nowadays, a Lexus.

Some hitters step into the batter's box and customize it too. Roberto Clemente would sweep his spikes over the dirt of the box to smooth out a surface. In doing so, he'd obliterate the back chalk line of the box so he could position himself in his favorite spot which, technically, was *out* of the box, too deep to be legally situated. Other batters dig a small hole for their back foot to rest in.

Former Toronto manager Cito Gaston said that Albert Belle "looks like he kinda' lines himself up in the batter's box by putting one foot in front of the other. Then he backs off and draws a line." Manny Sanguillen, former Pirates catcher, did basically the same thing. He'd enter the box, hold the bat by the barrel end, and draw a line in the dirt with the knob of the bat, parallel to the plate.

Many batters go through rituals as they enter the box or even between swings, but none as extreme as Mike "The Human Rain Delay" Hargrove or Nomar Garciaparra. They are as fidgety as a little boy harnessed by a starched shirt in Sunday school. Butch Hobson knew that it was just a way of getting comfortable, but marveled at Hargrove's habits. "He used to do his batting glove—step out, mess with his glove, every pitch."

Flashy infielder Tito Fuentes entered his comfort zone in the box by showboating. Joe Torre recalled, "He did the baton thing with his bat." Fuentes would even take his stick and bounce it off home plate, flamboyantly catching it as it ricocheted up to him.

Sparky Anderson observed of Jesus Alou, "He used to do his neck [stretching and craning it] all the time." Again, just a way to become comfortable.

People, especially announcers, made a big deal of the preswing mannerisms of batters such as Joe Morgan, with the chicken-wing flapping of his back arm, or Stargell's windmill rotation of his bat. Gaston mused, "People have their mannerisms; I don't think the majority are superstitions. I think it's just something they do. Everybody has little keys to keep themselves mechanically sound."

Hargrove reflected on Morgan: "Every time I saw him do that, I thought it was something to remind him to keep his elbow down." In truth, almost every big-league hitter has a part of his body in motion prior to the pitch as a sort of technique to overcome the inertia of a dead standstill at the plate.

Some players often change their stance or swing. A 1999 article on Cal Ripken Jr. in USA *Today/Baseball Weekly* referred to his "Man of a Thousand Stances" persona. Ripken said of his style, "Hitting has always been a feel, not so much a look for me." He said that he was always ready, then, to "try tinkering a little bit to get that feel."

He made it clear that there were many different starting points for his swing over the years, but that ultimately his stances were "designed to get my body to stay on the ball and not fly open." He also believed that while the starting points may have been drastically different, at the point of contact with the ball his swing remained the same.

Selby understood what Ripken was doing: "The game's all adjustments. People make adjustments everyday. If a guy's hot one week, you can bet there are scouts in the stands watching him, seeing what pitches he's hitting, and so you come into a different city or another team comes into town, they've got a scouting report on how to pitch you. Then you've got to make an adjustment. I think with Cal Ripken playing every day and going through fatigue and through the mental roller coaster that you go through, it was constant adjustments. I think he was the epitome of a well-adjusted baseball player."

Still, isn't it unusual for a superstar to alter his stance so much? Selby replied, "Some guys never change, and some guys feel like they have to change. He changed and it worked: he's a Hall of Famer. I think each player's different. That's the originality of the game and the uniqueness of each player in that some guys feel like they change stances, they feel better this way, or they don't. Some guys will go the whole season the same way and watch video and feel like they need to make a little adjustment, and some guys stay the same way their whole career. [Ripken] was just a superstar who made adjustments, and that prolonged his career, and it made him as great as he is."

Ripken worked as hard as anyone did at his trade. During a period late in his career, he went through three new stances over a period of about three seasons. These were not signs of weakness or panic. Upshaw explained, "Everybody from time to time changes his stance, usually in a small way. I think Cal's changes were relatively small." Making adjustments and keeping fresh may have been Cal's way of staying motivated, suggested Upshaw.

Plus, there was no doubt that as he aged he made adjustments. His stance circa August of 1999, for example, allowed him, said Ray Miller, his manager back then, to "use his hands instead of his body so much. When you get older, I think you experiment a little bit and start trying to generate power with your body."

Upshaw likened Ripken's changes, in one regard, to the approach Canseco once took. "He had two or three different stances. He had his power stance, a line-drive stance, and he had a two-strike crouch. It depends on what kind of swing they want to take [sometimes]." And, at times, the stance may vary depending upon who's on the hill. At times a hitter such as Ripken may be "having trouble getting around on the ball so they change to help their timing mechanism again."

As a rule, Selby said, typical adjustments made by hitters aren't necessarily huge ones but, rather, ones made to "scouting reports, where pitchers pitch you, the way [for pitchers] hitters hit off you—you might be tipping your pitches; it's all adjustments."

A great clutch hitter, in 1990 the 37-year-old George Brett became the first man to win batting crowns in three different decades. However, his season didn't start out auspiciously. By May 7, he was the recipient of lusty boos as his average had swan dived to .200. Brett, after deep consideration, changed his stance. "I opened up a little bit and put the bat up more on my shoulder," he said.

His turnabout was as rapid as it was miraculous, as he hit over .350 from that point on and over .380 after the All-Star break. "When I started to hit after the break, I said to myself, 'Hey, I can still hit.'"

Men like Brian Downing and, more recently, and *much* more drastically, Tony Batista have extremely wide open stances. Such a stance allows both eyes to face the pitcher directly, aiding, some say, in depth perception. In a closed stance, the eye farther away from the pitcher doesn't get as good a look at the pitch coming in. And still, it's estimated that around 90 percent of big leaguers use a closed stance.

Batista, who has perhaps the most exaggerated open stance ever, begins his stance by seemingly facing the pitcher with both legs and with both eyes. Although he alters that stance as he gets into his hitting mode, it remains a strange sight, but it works for him. In 2002 he popped 31 homers and drove in 87 runs.

In 2000, Frank Thomas also went the route he said he had seen paved by Batista and Galarraga, opening his stance quite a bit. When he did so, he was immediately delighted, saying, "Once I made the adjustment, I was like a kid with a new toy. It was just time for a change." He added, "When something isn't working anymore, I don't care how much pride you have, it's time to change."

Unlike Gwynn and his consistency with his stance and spot in the box, Rod Carew would adjust his stance against certain pitchers or in certain situations. Thus, he might have an open stance versus a pitcher early in the game and closed later in that same contest.

Even to a fan who was unfamiliar with Wade Boggs, who had never read the back of his bubble-gum card, Boggs's very stance indicated he was a contact hitter and was not too concerned with lofting balls for homers, as today's hitters often do. He held his hands pretty much in front of him, not coiled back behind his body. From that stance Boggs, not unlike Gwynn, would slash singles to left using his inside-out cut, often aiming at Fenway's Green Monster when he wore a Red Sox uniform.

For most big-league hitters, the perfect stride is rather short, about eight to twelve inches. Bagwell's stride is more like eight to twelve millimeters, *if that*. At least one broadcaster has said Bagwell's front foot does not actually stride toward the pitcher—he raises the foot, but places it back down in almost exactly the spot where it originally rested—quite unusual. Some batters, of course, simply don't fit into the bell-shaped curve of human endeavor. Few hitters have taken a stance with feet as far apart as Bagwell does; it's a puzzle as to how he generates such power from such a "base" of his wide-spread feet.

Yankees great Don Mattingly willingly admitted that his stance and swing were far from being textbook perfect. "I have a strange stance," he began. "My front foot is probably in the wrong place and I inside-out too many balls, but I get the job done."

Another interesting swing belonged to Dave Justice. Dawson noted, "He has that real nice and easy stroke, and the ball just seems to jump off his bat, too. He's one of the bigger guys, and with that stroke he generates a lot of bat speed."

Meanwhile, World Series hero Joe Carter admired power-hitting McGriff's swing. "Freddie has got that big, huge backswing—where he swings, he gets lift, and he hits the ball to left field [his opposite field], and he just sits there with that big follow-through. He's the only guy I know who can hit the ball out of all parts of the field and sit at home plate and watch it. I can watch 'em when I hit the ball to left-center or left field [pulling the ball], but if I hit one to right field, I don't know if it's gone or not. He is probably one of *the* strongest guys in baseball as far as hitting the ball out of the ballpark. He's got a lot of raw talent."

The McGriff swing is also surprisingly powerful according to Andre Dawson, who felt that what separated McGriff from the rest was his swing. "He amazes me because he doesn't even seem to swing very hard and the ball jumps off his bat. Most of his home runs are tape-measure shots and when he's swinging the bat real well, he's a joy to watch." Mickey Tettelton agreed, adding, "He hits 'em where most guys need a driver or a three wood to get to."

Speaking of backswing, when it comes to the completion of the swing, a relatively new trend in baseball features the high follow-through which Rettenmund said adds lift to the ball. Hitting the ball hard with the Brady Anderson–like follow-through results in a lot of home runs. Rettenmund thinks Gary Sheffield could add even more homers to his total if his finish wasn't a bit flat.

At any rate, it's clear that there's a great deal of diversity in baseball when it comes to hitters' stances, swings, and even mannerisms. It's hard to fathom that so many different approaches actually work, but they do.

10

Equipment: The Tools of Hitting

FROM THE VERY first Louisville Slugger bat to be branded with a player's signature—Honus Wagner—up through today, bats are very special to hitters.

Enos Slaughter said he always knew when he had selected the proper bat. "When a bat feels right, the balance is so perfect it feels weightless. I spent my whole career looking for a bat that felt as good as the broom handles I used to play stickball." Of course Paul Waner once took a different viewpoint. He said, "It's not the bat that counts. It's the guy who's wielding it."

The rule book states that a big-league bat "shall be a smooth, rounded stick not more than 2¾ inches in diameter at the thickest part and not more than 42 inches in length." It goes on to declare that the bat must be one piece of solid wood. In addition, it even regulates the depth and width of the indentation of the now-popular cupped bats.

In 1880 a bat could even have four distinct sides rather than the round shape the game now knows. That freakish bat was soon banned.

Rules continued to evolve slowly, but there were times when a batter would still use a bat that was flat on part of one side.

Through the years some hitters have altered their bats illegally, trying to give themselves an edge — most notably by corking their bats. Typically the player will drill a hole in the end of his bat and fill it with cork, rubber, or even Superballs, all with the idea of making the bat more lively. Though players swear a juiced bat will cause long outs to become home runs, some scientists say that's simply not true.

Perhaps if a player believes he has an advantage by swinging a loaded bat, then in his mind he does. On June 3, 2003, a badly slumping Sammy Sosa joined the ranks of players such as Graig Nettles (who packed his bat with Super Balls), Albert Belle, Wilton Guerrero, Chris Sabo, Billy Hatcher, and Jose Guillen (who was caught during a minor-league rehab assignment using an illegal stick). Sosa denied knowledge of using the corked bat, but was suspended nevertheless.

Omar Vizquel, a teammate of Belle when he was caught, said, "If you use a bat like that, you have to be very careful." Mulholland pointed out that since the rule states a team can only check an opposing player's bat once in a game, that can open the door to more cheating. "Once you check one bat," he said, "nine guys are going to be scurrying to their lockers for Old Corky."

Former pitcher Steve Farr told Paul Hoynes of the *Cleveland Plain Dealer* that the Indians used to have a veritable wood-working shop at Cleveland Memorial Stadium. More cork was in evidence there than in a winery. Cleveland's expert at doctoring bats would insert the cork, then "use a wood burner to re-create the wood grain to hide his tracks," wrote Hoynes.

Farr also spoke of Ernie Camacho, ironically a pitcher, "putting mercury into the bats." Mulholland elaborated, "Players will drill a hole in a bat, put a metal tube in there and put mercury in the tube. When you swing the bat, the mercury rushes to the end of the bat and creates kinetic energy."

Baseball also regulates how far up the handle a material such as pine tar may cover or treat the bat to improve its grip. One of the most notorious examples of enforcement of this rule occurred on July 24, 1983, when George Brett hit what would have been a game-winning home run against Yankees star Goose Gossage with two outs in the ninth inning. Instead of celebrating, Brett went ballistic when the umpires ruled he had used an illegal bat, one that had heavy amounts of pine tar about 20 inches from the tip of the handle. An obscure rule stated, "The bat handle, for not more than 18 inches from the end, may be covered or treated with any material to improve the grip." Brett's bat violated the rule, and the umpires called him out.

Brett fumed, in part, because, as he put it, "I was aware of the rule, but I thought that it couldn't go past the label. Some umpires today, when they see the pine tar too high will say, 'Hey, George, clean up your bat.' I don't wear batting gloves," he continued. "I like the feel of raw skin on raw wood. But you also don't want to hold the bat where pine tar is, so you put it up higher on the bat, get some on your hands when you need it, and then go back to the bottom of the bat."

(For the record, the league president overruled the umps, and the home run stood. The game was ordered replayed from the moment of the homer, and Brett's Royals finally prevailed.)

In reality, no matter what limitations the rule book lists, bats used by major leaguers today seldom are longer than 36 inches and, according to hitting coach Duane Espy, the norm is about 34 inches and 32 ounces. "That's middle of the road," he said. "That's the average. I don't think the heavy bat is much in existence any more. It was a very common thing not too long ago, but now I would say that it is definitely a rarity. Whether the player is a slap hitter or a power guy or whatever, heavy bats have kind of gone by the wayside."

Players of the early era loved heavy bats. Bill Williams of the Hillerich and Bradsby Company, producers of the famous Louisville Slugger line of bats, said, "In the past, players used much heavier bats. Babe Ruth used 40-ounce bats in 1927 when he hit 60 homers." His original 1914 bat weighed in at a cumbersome 48 ounces. He even took cuts with a 50-ounce bat, but it is believed he only had that bat for practicing. Some have said that the great Ruth once wielded a 56-ounce bat.

Heavy bats were often made of hickory. Thick-handled bats, including ones with milk-bottle barrels, were also popular. No matter the conventions of the era, bat selection all boils down to a matter of individual preference and what feels good to the hitter.

A few examples: Roger Maris used a 33-ounce bat when he broke Ruth's single-season home-run record of 60, hitting 61 in 1961. One source says Ruth actually used a 47-ounce hickory bat for the majority of his record-setting homers. He dropped down to a 36-ounce weapon for his final year in the majors.

By the 1960s when Philadelphia's Dick Allen carried a 40-ounce bat to the plate, his peers considered that to be a very heavy bat. Eddie Murray's weapon of choice was a 36-inch, 36-ounce bat. Interestingly, Hank Aaron, the all-time home-run king, was comfortable with 31- and 32-ounce bats. Further, according to physicist and author Robert K. Adair, no hitter since Ruth, with the exceptions of Ernie Lombardi (and Allen), seems to have used a bat over 40 ounces in the majors.

About the only contemporary player who comes close to using a bat of that weight is Garret Anderson of the Anaheim Angels. Unafraid to swing a heavy 35-ounce bat, Anderson is confident he can turn on virtually any pitcher's best fastball.

Bats in the early era of the game also tended to be quite long. Nap Lajoie, an Indians star, used a 35½-inch-long bat that weighed 34 ounces, while Tris Speaker's bat went 34½ inches and weighed in at 40 ounces. One of Ruth's hefty bats measured a substantial 36 inches long.

As noted in Chapter 9, many batters from that era choked up on their long bats. Merv Rettenmund, who, as also noted previously, does not advocate choking up on the bat, recognizes that choking up works for Barry Bonds. "He orders his bats," observed Rettenmund, "to fit that swing of his. It looks like it's a bat without a knob, and he has a very, very short swing—I mean, it is unbelievably good."

While he doesn't know what percentage of major leaguers currently choke up, he did say that "a lot of bats are designed, like the C271, which is a really popular model right now, [in such a way that] to hold the bat at the smallest area, you have to choke up about three-quarters of an inch. But, if you want good bat control, you can also spread your hand—like Ty Cobb used to do, but not *that* much. To control the barrel a little better, you could spread them a little bit."

While many old bats had very wide barrels that didn't taper or thin off much toward the handle, today's players like bats with thin handles. Espy said there are now "all kinds of styles of bats and shapes and sizes. There are still some guys who use the no-knob [bat]." Still, overall he went along with the belief that the thin handles far outnumber the thick ones, but when it comes to the barrels, "you see everything from the small ones to the big ones and everything in between."

Andres Galarraga, who has hit as high as .370, said, "I like a 35/33 bat [35 inches and 33 ounces]. Sometimes 35/34. It depends on the pitcher. When the pitchers throw hard," he said in a 2002 interview, "I go with 34 or 34-and-a-half [ounces]. When the pitcher throws more breaking balls, I'm going 35/34."

As the season wears on, a player tends to wear down. When that occurs, a hitter may switch to a lighter bat. Galarraga said, "Sometimes I come down an ounce—like from 34 to 33, sometimes from 34-and-a-half to 33-and-a-half. It depends."

While such a slight difference may seem infinitesimal or even absurd to an amateur, to a pro there *is* a difference. "Yes, big time," he emphasized, "because we play every day. It's a long season, and that time of year [the dog days of the season] you get a little tired, so you have to work on ways to keep your body going. One ounce *can* make a difference in the swing sometimes."

Ted Williams said he'd weigh his bats often because they can gain a slight amount of weight just by picking up dirt from the ground or from condensation. Favoring a light bat (usually 33 ounces), he didn't want his bats adding even a single ounce. Such attention to detail, very Cobb-like, may be called obsessive-compulsive by critics or, more generously, the act of a perfectionist.

Selby listed the reasons he will change bats during the year. "Sometimes, physically, you're a little tired; you feel like you might want to go to a lighter bat. Sometimes you can be in the middle of a slump and a different model feels better—that's just [your] tools; some things feel better. A lot of times fatigue plays a bit part in it." So, as scientific as the game has become, the selection of bats often reverts back to what "feels good."

Selby declared that when he does change bats, it's always a change in weight. "I've never changed my length; it's always been 34 inches, but I think a lot of guys do [change the length]. Some guys use longer bats, or bigger, heavier bats, [against] guys who throw a lot of breaking balls. Some guys use lighter bats when they feel like they really need to get to a ball. I don't think anybody is going to change more than an inch if they change the length of their bat."

Like fatigue, age is another factor when it comes to selecting a bat. Some players downsize over the course of their career. It's reported that Cobb began his career wielding a 40-ounce bat but finished with a still-solid 35-ounce stick. Former American League MVP Fred Lynn commented, "When I was 18, I used a big bat and I could pull anybody. Now [in his 11th season] I'm down about four ounces to a 31-ounce bat. But late in the season I've gone down to 29 ounces."

According to hitting instructor Bernardo Leonard, the bat of preference among major leaguers is one with a wide grain, since those with thin grain "will splinter and crack more quickly. If it's wide, the bat has been made with the best part of the tree. If there are any knots in the barrel head of the bat, the bat has been made from the hardest part of the wood." Carew tried to use bats with the streaks from the grain far apart, but would also harden his bats just as players from the era of Cobb did. He would rub the bat, with the grain, using a butcher's bone to compress the wood.

While hitters traditionally used bats made of white ash, things are now changing. Bonds became enamored of bats made of sugar maple, saying it felt harder and stronger and caused the balls to leap from his bat with more authority than before. Even when he got jammed inside, he'd muscle a single to the outfield rather than wind up with a broken-bat pop fly-out. By mid-1999 he abandoned ash bats, and in 2001 his new stick helped him leave all former home-run records in the dust when he launched 73 long-balls.

Batters choose their weapons not only after considering size, weight, and feel, but some have said they carefully pick even the color of the bat. There's a theory that using a dark bat helps outfielders pick up the ball quickly off the bat since the white of the ball contrasts nicely with the dark bat, helping the defender's eyes. With that in mind, and looking to put the defense at a disadvantage, those who hold to that theory choose light-colored sticks.

The sweet spot on the bat, the area where hitters love to meet and tear into a ball, is about 10 inches long out on the barrel of the bat. There are stories of men such as Williams whose bat had a small cluster of marks on the sweet spot from where they had hit so very many balls, and very few markings anywhere else on the bat; these stars made their living by hitting the ball on the sweet spot.

Players are often very protective of their bats. Espy said, "There are some guys who don't want anybody messing with them; they have to put them in certain places. Then there are other guys who [aren't so intense]. I think it's kind of an individualistic thing. But some guys are very particular about what happens to their bats, where they're at, and how they're used—[if] other people are using them."

Before the corked-bat incident, it was reported that Sosa let nobody touch his bats, storing them in his Fort Knox of a locker. Rose is said to have been so protective of his bats that he toted them around himself, trusting no one else with them.

Hitters are much more protective of their gamers, the bats they use during games, as opposed to those used in batting practice. David Justice, for one, often had game bats slip out of his hands. When one sailed into the stands, invariably he'd send a batboy to retrieve it, giving the fan a different bat as a reward.

One unnamed, but very good, hitter made it clear that he'd share his bats with any player on the team who wanted to try them out—except for pitchers. He forbade any pitcher from touching, and thus jinxing, his timber. Yet another superstitious old-timer felt that his bats contained only so many hits. Naturally, such thinking prohibited him from lending out his bats.

Jose Macias is one hitter who doesn't mind sharing his bats at all. "I always say if anybody needs my bat, they can use it. A lot of guys use my bat; they say, 'Oh, man, this bat feels comfortable.'" In a way, he feels that letting regulars borrow his bats is a small way he can contribute to the team effort. So, Macias, realizing he may be helping his team out, not to mention the fact that the bats are free, is generous.

He tells teammates, "You want to use it and you're hitting good—use it." He also said that sometimes he'd pick up another player's bat, and suddenly that one just felt right. Players tend to reciprocate.

In case a teammate breaks one of his bats, Macias has backups. That's important because when he was with Montreal it sometimes took quite a while for new bats to make their way from the factory to the ballpark—as long as three weeks to cross the border and into Canada, he said. He said that the Raleigh and Easton bats, shipped from a Canadian firm, ironically took longer to reach him, but the Louisville ones came relatively quickly.

Around 2002, Sosa began using a unique bat featuring an oversized knob. "I've got a theory on that [bat]," said Espy. "We made up some training bats one year when I was with the Giants and put huge wooden knobs on them that were a couple of inches below your hands and big around [like Sosa's]. It was a kind of experimental thing. I don't know if he's taken that same idea and used it, but it was a counterweight. You put weight below your hands, and when you release the bat it should move the bat head faster because there's weight underneath your hands."

Although none of the players Espy worked with used the bat during games, he said they liked it. "The bats were 40 ounces, but because X amount of the weight was below your hands, it actually felt like a 30- or 31-ounce bat. It actually felt light even though it was a much heavier bat."

Players in recent years have also altered the barrel end of their bats. "You take a bat that's maybe 34 or 35 ounces, and you take two ounces out of the end of it that you're not going to use," began Espy. "Now you've got a 32-ounce bat but it's 35-ounce wood. I think it's smart."

McGwire liked to use his bat to play soft toss. His coach would lob the ball underhanded, and Big Mac would diligently pound pitch after pitch into a net. It took less than two dozen cuts for him to get a feel for his bat and his swing and to prepare for another day at the office.

Whether an on-deck hitter swings a lead bat, a device that resembles a stick with four 1950s-like automobile fins, or a sledgehammer, the idea is simply to loosen up with a heavier object than the game bat. After taking cuts with a bat with a weighted sleeve, for example, the game bat feels light and easy to swing as the hitter steps up to the plate. Espy commented, "Mostly it's just getting loose, getting the feel of something heavier [with] resistance, and then taking that off and having your bat feel light in your hands."

Speaking of the feel of the bat, Willie Upshaw, who served as a hitting coordinator with the Cleveland Indians' player development program, can remember when batting gloves weren't in vogue. "I never did [wear them] until one spring training when I got blisters. I didn't want to quit hitting so I got used to them."

Long ago it wasn't unusual for players' early spring swings to be impaired by raw, bloody hands. Jeromy Burnitz of the Dodgers said the batting glove has evolved greatly. "When they first started wearing gloves, they were wearing work gloves, and the technology has developed and gloves help. I mean, you can play the game without 'em, but obviously they've discovered that they help, and just through time, here we are — everybody's using them."

Reportedly, Ken Harrelson actually was the first player to use gloves to protect his hands, which were raw from having played too many rounds of golf on a game day. Some say he actually used golf gloves at first, not work gloves.

Burnitz said he uses gloves because "the problem for me is gripping the bat. You start sweating. It's not about blisters. We can all get our hands tough enough to grip the bat, but I let the bat fly as it is, so I gotta have them." Players tend to wear them for a better grip especially on hot, humid days. However, in some cases they wear them for the lucrative endorsements that glove companies dish out.

Upshaw believes that players today could at times do without them, and some players do. Most players today wear two batting gloves, but as recently as the days of Dale Murphy some players, including the two-time MVP, took to wearing only one glove.

Mark Grace contends he gets a better feel for the bat without gloves. A throwback to the old days, he seldom wears a glove. When he does, it's usually to protect his hands against the cold. He told *Sports Illustrated* that instead of gloves, he uses "a lot of pine tar and a lot of rosin, and it makes for a good grip. I just don't like batting gloves—you can't get a good feel for the bat. I like the feel of wood." Minnesota's Doug Mientkiewicz is another rarity who eschews batting gloves, wearing only a gold glove on defense.

Although the average fan associates protective padding in the batter's box with Barry Bonds, he certainly is not the only batter to wear the bulky, protective guards on his arm (or even over the hand). Brady Anderson is widely recognized as the first player to wear the Rollerblade elbow pad that soon was used by hitters such as Andres Galarraga and Alex Rodriguez. Soon, batters began to suit up like an Arthurian knight.

"When you get hit on the elbow, even if it doesn't chip, it's going to at least be difficult to swing," Anderson explained in *USA Today/Baseball Weekly* in August 1998. "I'm going to stand wherever I want and not move anyway. This just helps prevent injuries."

Mo Vaughn and Bonds began to use more elaborate body armor, and it became an accepted, if not standard, part of the game. After some time, though, more than a few pitchers began to grumble that the armor-clad hitters were taking the inside part of the plate away from them and were diving into pitches with no trepidation of being hit. If pitchers worked hitters over the plate or on the outside corner, the hitters would drive the ball, fully extending their mighty arms. Not only that, pitches that normally were called strikes, nipping the inside corner, now appeared to be tight on the plate-hugging hitters.

In the same article, Houston's Craig Biggio, who donned an elbow guard, said, "I've always felt that half of the plate is mine and half of it is the pitcher's." He contended that if he was hanging out over the plate and got hit, so be it. Of course, pitchers could counter this argument by saying, "That's easy for him to say; he'll get first base for free and it won't even hurt him."

Biggio did say that the protective equipment felt awkward but was worth it. "If you get hit in the elbow or tricep, it's going to affect your swing for a week," he said. Bagwell agreed that if such equipment is available and helps a hitter, why not wear it. He not only didn't want to get injured, he didn't want to miss any playing time. In his case, his logic was entirely understandable: he had a fractured bone in his left hand once in 1993 and twice in 1994. That cinched it for him; a special protective device was sewn into his batting glove for that hand.

Some have proposed that if a batter is hit on arm padding, the pitch would be called a ball or strike depending upon its location; however, the hitter would not be awarded first base. If the pitch hits him in an unprotected area, then, as has always been the case, he would be awarded first.

Cleveland announcer Matt Underwood says he and his fellow announcers have discussed the topic of such gear. "We've talked about it on the air before. The Boston guys were some of the first ones that did it, [like] Mo Vaughn. They'd really hang out over [the plate]. The problem is that Vaughn's elbow is in the strike zone, so you start to wonder—if he gets hit in the strike zone, that should be a strike. It's really plain and simple. Another idea is to just outlaw body armor altogether and see if these guys hang out over the plate," said the broadcaster. However, as long as hitters can use the protection, they will continue to try to own the strike zone.

The length of pads is limited, yet Brent Butler says, "Some of them look bigger, but some guys [can] wear them for medical reasons. Other guys wear them because that's a real tender place [the elbow] to get hit by a 90-plus-mile-an-hour fastball. Some guys wear them just so they don't have to miss a week or two of play from getting smoked in the elbow."

The advantage of crowding the plate is enormous. In 2002 when Toby Harrah was serving as a coach for the Arizona Diamondbacks, he said he felt that gaining such an edge wasn't fair, that it gave hitters a fearlessness at the plate. However, when asked if he would have worn such guards, his playing-days instinct came out. He conceded, "Absolutely. I'd have been a little bit closer to the plate, too, and covered that ball on the outside corner a little bit more. Sixty percent of the pitches that are thrown are basically away, to the outside part of the plate. So, if you can cover that part of the plate, you're going to help yourself as a hitter.

"I remember it used to be a guy hit a home run, the next guy got dropped or got drilled or got pitched up and in. Now if you throw a ball inside to a hitter, he's ready to fight." Even though hitters may be wearing protection, they still aggressively protect the inside part of the plate, willing to fight at the drop of, well, a bat.

Since numerous pitchers have come to accept the convention of the day—not to pitch batters tight—hitters have gained two advantages: they can crowd the plate, and, again, even if they get hit, it won't hurt.

As a former position player, Harrah elaborated: "For me, the biggest thing that I have a problem with is all the protective gear now that hitters are wearing at the plate. It used to be if you stood on the plate, you had to take your medicine, but nowadays with all the protective gear—I mean if they'd had that stuff a long time ago, I think I may have hit 100 more home runs. Now you can hang over the plate, and if they throw you inside and drill you, you [the pitcher] get warned. I guess maybe it's a pretty good idea [to wear such gear]. But myself, I would rather see if they wanted to change anything, it would be to take all that protective gear away, and maybe wear something on your ankle where you're going to foul a ball off. But as far as wearing stuff on your elbow and arm, I don't like to see that."

Why has the game changed from the days of Don Drysdale, who would plunk a batter as quickly and with as little thought as he would plunk down a nickel to buy a candy bar, to an era now when pitchers have become timid? Harrah replied, "I think umpires now seem to warn pitchers more than before. It used to be the umpires would let a lot of things slide and one guy'd get hit on one team, then a guy would get drilled on the other team, and then pretty much everything was even. Nowadays there seems to be a lot less of that, and there are more warnings. I think maybe they're just trying to protect the players more than ever before. Maybe it's because they're making more money."

Harrah said that while the protective equipment is restricted to a certain length, "I think there might be some Grandfather Rule in there, where if you've been wearing a pad in the past, you can continue to wear it." He was only partially correct.

According to Matt Gould, major-league baseball's Manager of Media Relations, "The pads are limited to 10 inches in length when measured with the pad lying flat. A player can wear a nonstandard elbow protective pad that does not meet those regulations only after receiving approval from the Office of the Commissioner. Part of the approval process includes a physician's report or letter that identifies the player, his injury, and the proposed pad and a photo measuring the pad or a sample of the pad." Once the letter is evaluated, the commissioner makes a ruling. If he approves the pad, then the player may begin to wear the protection.

"The physician is also requested to estimate the length of time the pad will be necessary," added Gould. In theory, if a player had a chronic condition, he could wear padding indefinitely, but the commissioner takes such matters on a case-by-case basis.

There can be ramifications for using nonstandard gear. Gould commented, "If a club has a complaint about a protective elbow pad, the team would alert the umpire working the game that night, and an umpire's report would be filed with the Commissioner's Office regarding that complaint, and an investigation will be undertaken. It would begin the day the umpire's report was received. If the player is found to have used the nonstandard elbow pad without approval, the [offending] club is subject to discipline." While there is no defined penalty, the ruling would, again, be on a case-by-case basis.

Even hitters' hats have been scrutinized by baseball experts. The colors of the lining under the bill of the cap have been studied, with certain colors deemed better for players' eyes. Typically, green, black, or gray colors have been used for the caps. Richie Sexson commented, "I've heard of that before, but I had never really thought about it. I think Orel Hershiser was one who was really big on that. He didn't like the light color under the hat for some reason—it did something with his eyes—but I never really noticed the difference. I've played with white underneath, and gray, and black. I think now, for the most part, most of them are black." He grabbed two of his hats, and verified that one was gray and one was black.

Finally, here is a tip on equipment for young players. Hall of Famer Frank Robinson advised, "If I were a kid going to college and had an idea of playing professional baseball, I would buy my own wooden bats." Using aluminum may pad a college player's stats, but the numbers are misleading. For a true gauge of ability and to get used to using the equipment of the pros, Robinson recommends using a wooden bat.

11

Hitting Coaches and Their Philosophies

TRIS SPEAKER WAS once asked how he accounted for his hitting prowess. He replied, "It would be useless for any player to attempt to explain successful batting." Of course that hasn't stopped countless coaches from trying to do just that: explain the unexplainable.

One thing is for sure, though: a good hitting coach can be a godsend. He knows a player's stance and style and will diligently watch his every move during every single at-bat. He can sometimes pick up a problem that even the hitter can't see or feel. Too, the coach might notice a trend concerning how the batter is being pitched. When the hitter returns to the dugout, the coach might comment, "Did you notice how he worked you away on your first at-bat, but this time he started coming in on you?" Or, "Your hips flew open on that last swing."

George Bernard Shaw may have felt very clever—even smug—when he wrote, "He who can, does. He who cannot, teaches." It is true that one of the most highly respected batting coaches of all time, Charlie Lau, was a career "can't-do" .255 hitter. It's also true that some standout managers were mediocre players, such as Sparky Anderson (until Hal Lanier broke his record, Anderson's 104 hits in a season were the fewest ever by a regular for a 154-game schedule), Walter Alston, and Tommy Lasorda. They are often cited as proof of Shaw's theory. However, some great hitters were also great teachers. Ted Williams, one of the greatest hitters ever (he once batted .406), was also a splendid mentor and batting guru.

Williams, to paraphrase an old baseball line, had forgotten more about hitting over the years than so many others would ever learn over a lifetime. One tangible evidence attesting to his skills came in 1969, Williams's first as the manager of the Washington Senators. After working with his offense, the team batting average shot up 27 points from the previous year.

Tom McCraw, who played for Williams, said that he was a great teacher of hitting. "Two years they [the Senators] did super well, offensively. He did a heck of a job bringing them [hitters] around. He knew what good hitting was about, and he got them to buy into it. They did, and they had some good years for him. He's why I'm a hitting instructor today." Williams opened "his mind up to me about what [hitting is] about. He taught hitting, and I was fortunate enough to be a recipient of some of his teachings."

For example, Williams knew, and therefore taught, that it was vital to know the strike zone and equally important to refuse to chase bad pitches. He told hitters that to increase the strike zone by just two inches off the plate was to increase the pitcher's target by a whopping 35 percent. Plus, if a hitter begins to go after outside stuff, the odds increase that pitchers will not give him offerings down the heart of the plate.

McCraw agrees that a coach can be effective whether he hit a ton as a player or not. It doesn't matter, says McCraw, if you learn the art of hitting. "There are some guys who are hitting instructors who can't teach it; they're just great hitters. Now, a guy like Lau, a guy like myself, and some others—we had to work at it, we had to learn by accident, or whatever. You learn some of the keys to what turns hitters on, what makes hitters click. You need the ability to relate; if you've got that ability, then you've got a chance to teach. And it's not about you, it's about the hitter and the basic things you need to do: 'Let's go one-on-one, let's work on them, let's get it done.'"

Rob Picciolo put the hitting coach–hitter relationship in an interesting frame. He felt that if a player is a bright, receptive student to a good hitting coach, the player just *has* to improve as a hitter. He gave credit to one of his great coaches, Billy Williams, himself a Hall of Fame–caliber hitter. "Billy helped me tremendously. I wasn't a great hitter, but I had a lot of people throw different philosophies out at me and try different things. A lot of it has to come from within, but there are guys who make suggestions. But it boils down to: when you're sitting in that box, you're pretty much on your own."

Despite stories of coaches having a pet project (Lau working with George Brett comes to mind) or a teacher's pet, most coaches say that they're proud of all their hitters. Duane Espy said he "feels good about anybody that does well — these guys are all the same to me. I'm trying for them to all hit well and have big nights every night. There's nobody that's more important to me than anybody else."

However, some hitters have a fierce loyalty for a particular hitting coach. When it was announced shortly after the 2002 season that the Royals had fired hitting coach Lamar Johnson, Mike Sweeney, the second leading hitter in the AL that year, said he was heartbroken. "For four-and-a-half years Lamar helped me get where I am today. If he can turn me into a good hitter, he can do anything."

In 2000 Todd Helton credited his hitting coach Clint Hurdle with helping his approach to the game. Helton said Hurdle taught him that the more you play, "the more you realize when to be aggressive and when the pitcher has to sort of pitch around you and not give you a good pitch to hit. Clint stressed that you've got to go up there and be aggressive, and if you get a first-pitch fastball, a good pitch to hit, there's nothing wrong with swinging and letting it go."

Michael Barrett also spoke of the importance of hitting coaches. "I think every hitting coach has their own signature lesson or skill. One thing that Mac [Expos coach Tom McCraw] has really taught me is: it's not about mechanics at this level, it's about how you're thinking, your mental approach at the plate to hitting — how you prepare yourself when you're in the dugout and on deck, that's what you're going to take with you up to the plate.

"If you're in the dugout or in the on-deck circle and you're thinking about a specific mechanic, when you go up to the plate it doesn't matter what your mechanic is. If you're not aware that that guy has a really good curveball, you're going to swing through it and miss it every time no matter how good your mechanics are.

"It's something that I really felt was the key to hitting, but I had a hitting coach the last couple of years who didn't go with that philosophy. [He] really felt that the key was mechanics—the key was staying on your legs so you could see the ball. I can see how both work, but some work better for other hitters." Staying on your legs, Barrett clarified, basically means staying down and balanced and maintaining that balance throughout the swing.

In Barrett's first year his hitting coach was former outfielder Tommy Harper. "He was more like McCraw, a guy that played in the big leagues a long time and was more on the mental approach of baseball. I had a chance to work with Bernie Carbo early on in my career—he was great for me. He brought a major-league approach to a small town that didn't really have a whole lot of knowledge about hitting other than the tapes that we could get hold of. We used to watch Charlie Lau hitting tapes all the time and read Ted Williams's book *The Science of Hitting*. We really studied those things back in [my home town] Alpharetta, Georgia."

He said that Carbo's ideas, while a little different from Lau's, were a great influence, nevertheless, giving him a different slant. "He was more of a Walt Hriniak style." Barrett felt the contrast between Hriniak and Lau "would be more the emphasis put on the legs and the balance. The finish is not important [to Hriniak]; one-handed or two-handed—you could do either one. It was more or less the [concept of] balance plus extension equals power. Barrett also recalled that Lau emphasized "head down to the ball, and more of a one-hand release. That would be his signature move—his philosophy. I'd say that probably produced more front-foot hitters and more hitters [hitting] for average."

A more detailed discussion of Lau and Hriniak, both light-hitting catchers, is in order. First of all, Lau was so convinced his theories could help any hitter, he once said that any major-league hitter should be able to hit safely at least once for every four of his at-bats, well above the embarrassing "Mendoza Line" of .215.

Lau emphasized weight shift, the rather drastic forward shifting of the hitter's center of gravity from the back leg to the front. In contrast, power-hitting Williams emphasized the rotation of the hips to create a sort of shift, thus generating his power. Since approximately 95 percent of all balls hit up in the air are easy outs, Lau was a proponent of swinging on a level plane, striving for line drives and doing so with the front arm being dominant in the swing.

Then, even if a batter doesn't hit the ball cleanly, his swing will probably produce a hard ground ball, not a harmless fly ball. Ground balls tend to get through the infield and/or advance runners (and score runners) more than flies. Hriniak, a Lau disciple, followed such thinking, as he did on most of Lau's theories, including using the entire field, and holding the bat a bit high, often about shoulder level, and at a 45- to 90-degree angle to the ground.

Hriniak liked the hitter's head to be down even on the follow-through, allowing the batter to see the ball as long as possible. He cited Boggs as the type of hitter who successfully did this. The principle is similar to a golfer taking his swing with his head down.

Lau also stressed a relaxed, loose stance coupled with a controlled stride, aimed right back at the pitcher. He always preached, "You have to shift the weight back in order to then go forward." This concept is the same as used in another type of swing—a playground swing. There, a child must go back by walking backwards a few steps (or being pulled back by a parent) before his momentum can shift forward. Lau's students would coil backward prior to stepping into and attacking the pitch. Further, his hitters tended to finish with their front arm finishing high. Lau wrote in his book *The Art of Hitting .300*, "The hitter must step first and swing second," adding that those who step and swing at the same time lose both power and the ability to hit for contact.

Hitters who listened to Lau tended to hit for higher averages, partly because they didn't just pull the ball. They also struck out less than hitters who, for example, would swing for power with uppercuts. Hitters like that didn't shift their weight as drastically and tended to have their rear arm more dominant. Of course, for many, including Williams, this was the best route to follow. Williams even justified his uppercut, saying it was necessary to offset the fact that the pitcher, since he delivers the ball from an incline, is throwing the ball in a downward direction. Sluggers usually meet the ball in front of the plate, earlier than the Lau hitters, and they do so with their hands held lower, ready to uncoil and upper-cut the ball.

Jaramillo gave his thoughts on Lau and Hriniak, "With Lau, it was keeping your head down, keeping your head still, getting in a good hitting position early, and then the weight shift was a big thing for him and the way you finished high when you finished with your swing." He compared it to the finish on a Brady Anderson swing but said Lau advocated ending maybe a little higher.

"Hriniak tried to follow the Lau way, too, but I think what Charlie really meant was a lot of the things that I'm trying to teach. He just had different names for them. I call it 'getting in the power position' and he called it 'getting in a launching position.' I saw George Brett do the same things fundamentally that you want any hitter to do. He was a line-drive hitter, and he used the whole field, which is what Lau wanted."

McCraw said, "Charlie Lau was a good hitting instructor, [but] Hriniak jumped on the bandwagon. I'll say this—if, in fact, Hriniak's theory was correct, then that means Mickey Mantle, Hank Aaron, Frank Robinson, Harmon Killebrew, Carl Yastrzemski—all these guys were wrong. But they're in the Hall of Fame."

McCraw felt Hriniak was teaching guys to have their head down on the ball and wound up having "guys swinging, throwing their rotator cuffs out of pocket. It's simple, I mean: if you want to see what good hitting is, watch guys like Tony Gwynn, Robinson, Mantle, Tony Oliva, guys that hit—they didn't do all that crap." He was referring to the cut that players like Anderson took, with one hand leaving the bat as the hitter concluded his "helicopter cut," with the bat up high over the shoulders. "A lot of guys have ruined their career doing that," he said.

Also, McCraw noticed that some hitting coaches jump on a player's coattail to give themselves an ego fix. "It would be like me coming in here [Montreal] saying, 'I really did a lot of work with Vladimir [Guerrero] and [Jose] Vidro.' Those guys were hitting .300 before I got here."

McCraw says his job is to bring along the rookies and unestablished hitters so that the superstars of a team, such as Guerrero, have a strong supporting cast. "My job is to help lesser hitters get to that [higher] level, so I took pride when I was the hitting instructor in Houston for four years [and worked with] Richard Hidalgo and Daryle Ward and Brad Ausmus and Bill Spiers, and these guys developed as hitters. They all upped their game offensively—not Baggy [Jeff Bagwell] and Biggio. Hell, they were doing their thing before that." According to McCraw, a hitting instructor who points to a superstar from his team and takes credit for that player's success is guilty of being self-serving (or simply lying).

Some hitting coaches pretty much let the superstars take care of themselves unless they ask for help. The soft-spoken Jaramillo says that's not his style. "I'm a hands-on guy. Doesn't matter to me if you're a Hall of Famer or if you're anybody, I'm assertive in what I do; I'm in charge of my program. We work it out. Raffy [Rafael Palmeiro] was a great hitter when he came here, as well as Alex [Rodriguez], but my job is to help them be more consistent—get them prepared. I know their swings and they trust me to tell them, 'Get there a little sooner. Slow it down,' or whatever it takes.

"So, it's just something small that I tell them, but I make sure that they're prepared and that they know what that pitcher's going to do, even though they already do. They've been around the league, but I make them watch the tape. I do whatever it takes for them. I adjust to them because my job is to try to help them get the most out of themselves anyway I can, and that's what I do."

Merv Rettenmund said that he thinks "the most important thing that I try to stress is that the mechanics of a swing have never really helped anyone out, and if you don't believe in yourself or your swing, you're wasting your time. If you have confidence in your swing and you are relaxed, you're able to focus and see the ball, and the swing seems to work out pretty good."

He also said that he felt that if the timing and getting ready to hit the ball are on time, then the mechanics will be perfect and "you don't have to swing hard. The best examples of that are guys like Bonds and Mark McGwire. His [McGwire's] last couple of years he did not swing that hard, and yet he hit [the ball] tremendous distances.

"It's like hitting a golf ball. I think more people golf, and more people are good golfers than good hitters. When you really hit a ball a long way, it's how nice and how smooth it is and the timing—how it all comes together. It's difficult in baseball to keep that timing together all the time."

McCraw said that he doesn't talk about his philosophy of hitting; instead, he talks about what good hitting is. "Number one is work ethics. That's the number one thing—you can't be afraid to work. I've been around some great hitters, and I've helped create a few guys who have got over the hump and became pretty good hitters, but the first thing you establish is work ethics—you've got to be willing to work to get there. It doesn't get too hot to work extra; it doesn't get too cold to work extra—if you want to get to the top.

"After that, you take BP and extra hitting. All that stuff is conditioning you for game conditions." He pointed out how foolish it is for a player to hit a lot but not work on anything specific in BP. "I say [to such players], 'What'd you do?'"

Then, imitating both sides of a conversation, McCraw continued, "'Well, I had a thousand swings.'

"'I know, but what'd you work on?'

"'Man, I was really hitting the ball hard.'

"'I know, but what'd you work on?' A thousand swings not working on anything is not worth a crap. You'd rather have him take 50 swings and work on some phase of hitting than take a thousand swings just to say, 'I took a thousand swings.'"

Terry Francona recalled "Hriniak was the major-league hitting instructor in Chicago when I was in the minor leagues. So I really wasn't around him that much to hear his philosophy. But the one thing—his work ethic was unbelievable. You know, when you take major-league hitters and you work as hard as they do, something good's going to come of it no matter what you're telling them."

Willie Upshaw, who has been a hitting coach at the big-league level, concurs about hard work, saying coaches' duties don't end when the game does. "There are things you do, especially when you're working closely with guys, like talk to guys, pat them on the back, and reinforce things— especially things they've done *well*. You pump up certain guys, and you might watch video after a game."

At times a hitting coach will watch video of certain hitters by himself, like a college student cramming before an exam, getting prepared for the next day. Other times, the coach will sit down with a player and go over the video together to provide him with immediate feedback. It all depends on the player, his personality, whether the player did well but needs some refinement, or whether he did poorly and needs some retooling.

Jaramillo ran through a typical, arduous day at the park. He arrives extremely early, in time to be in the batting cage around three-thirty. "We do some drills. We hit a lot of breaking pitches off the machine. Then from there, I have early work at three-forty for about 15 minutes with people I tell everyday to come in and hit early—like four or five guys [he targets] to get extra work.

"A lot of my guys love to hit, so sometimes when I say I've got early hitting, ten or twelve guys show up. They love to hit, so it's enjoyable working with my guys because they're dedicated and they prepare. You know, sometimes we don't get the results we want, but I know that the effort was there of being prepared and getting their drills in and it will pay off in the long run.

"Then I come back in [the clubhouse] and watch some films of the pitcher [starting that night for the opponents], go over my advance scout reports, but usually I take [the films home] at night, and I watch the pitcher that we're facing the next day. That way I'm prepared when I come to the park and I let [the hitters] know what this guy does." He says that studying the night before helps him the next day when he already has more than enough to work on with his extremely tight time schedule.

As for the scouting reports, he said, "I take the advance report sheet individually to each one of the hitters, and we go over it because [for example] they're going to pitch Rafael Palmeiro different from the normal left-hander." He feels, then, that it is well worth the time and effort to go over the report player-by-player.

"Then we go out and hit, and I'm in the cage during that time. We have four groups of hitters, and we do drills and we talk about the pitcher. We rotate those four groups, but I stay in the [indoor] cage and not outside.

"At six-fifteen I have my little program with Alex Rodriguez that we go through, getting him ready. He does tee work, he hits breaking balls, he hits live hitting, and he wants situations, and he gets himself ready for the game until about five till seven in our cage." When done with the daily

A-Rod Show, it's nearly time for the opening pitch, time to gather up what he'll need with him on the bench during the game and tread down to the dugout.

Before the season began, back in spring training, the same sort of routines had begun. There, the hitters want, above all else, one thing from their hitting coaches, and that's plenty of time in the batting cages. Upshaw said the main goal is to "make sure the regulars are getting as much hitting as they want, on the field and in the cage for extra BP." He explained that there are a lot of players up from the minors clogging the spring training fields, but the regulars, naturally, come first.

Another vital job of a hitting coach is to observe players hitting—either in BP or during a game, looking for flaws. Although McCraw says that to a trained eye this task is easy, it is also highly important. "You look at a lot of different things. I can look at a swing and almost tell that you were swinging at something you weren't looking for, which tells me you didn't have a plan to hit. I look to see if your rhythm is right, see if you're jumping or if you're gliding nicely. That's from years of observation."

Sometimes the advice from a coach is deceptively simple. Jim Frey said the hitting advice he gave to Brett was "Attaway to hit, George." On a more serious note, when McCraw was asked what special instructions he would give to a rookie prior to his first at-bat against an overpowering pitcher such as Randy Johnson, he replied, "Do what you want to do. He's got a great fastball, he's got a great slider, so you know what he has, but [a hitter] has to do what he does. He has to look for the pitch he hits best, not for the one you might throw.

"As a matter of fact, you've got a tough slider, then I'm going to try to kick your ass before you get to that pitch. Because I know once you get to that pitch, my chances diminish tremendously. So, it's not a matter of what a pitcher throws, it's a matter of what I want to hit—until two strikes."

Jaramillo's view of the subject is to have faith in the hitters. "I think you just got to let them go up there and bring what they've brought with them from the minor leagues that they've had success with, and just leave them alone, let them play, and see how they adjust, then go from there.

"I mean, you're not trying to put anything in their heads because they just got here, so just let them play, and then when you see something, share it. They know what I tell them; they've been hearing it in the minor leagues anyway, so it's not going to be anything that's off base at all."

Under such situations, Rettenmund gives concise advice. He noted, "I think the game plan has to be pretty simple. Let's just use [facing] Curt Schilling as an example, but I think this would go with any of them, really: Look for the fastball out over the plate, obviously; if it's a hittable fastball, be ready and hit it right from the get-go. You're not up there taking. You know a lot of people think [that's the way to go now with] Oakland—taking a lot of pitches like the Rickey Hendersons have done to work the count, get into the count—but when you start mentioning pitchers like Schilling, if you want to let him get ahead of you 0-1, go ahead, and then you're going to be coming back to the bench."

To watch a fastball soar by for strike one is to place the pitcher in command. And against a great pitcher, good luck trying to figure what pitch you will see and where it will be thrown when that pitcher is on top of the count.

In the 2002 World Series the Angels faced the Giants' Livan Hernandez in Game 3. With the input of hitting coach Mickey Hatcher, they devised a strategy of attack that was, ironically, based on inactivity. Hatcher, knowing his players were good contact hitters, said he noticed from watching tapes that Hernandez often flirted with the strike zone by throwing pitches just off the plate. Hatcher said, "We wanted to make him throw pitches until he got the ball over the plate." It was part of a plan the Angels employed to make pitchers work hard while getting a feel for what the pitchers want to do against them on a given day.

Hatcher also said the Angels excel in battling at the plate and focus on moving runners up. They worked on the latter skill diligently in 2002, beginning in spring training. It paid off when they knocked out Hernandez quickly in the third contest, and it certainly paid off when they won it all just a few nights later.

Eddie Perez is most closely linked with the Braves' pitchers he caught for years. However, every NL ballplayer is also a hitter, and Perez has worked hard on that facet of his game. The coach that helped him the most was Stargell. "He was working with us one year and he helped me a lot," he said. "I think he was the guy who taught [hitting] to Dave Justice. When Dave was there [in Atlanta], he wasn't hitting that much, but then

Willie got there and he exploded. He won the Rookie of the Year." Stargell actually had helped hitters such as Perez and Justice even during their minor-league days.

As for Stargell's strategic impact on Perez: "The first thing I remember was that he [taught me] to hit the ball to right center field. I never did that in the minor leagues, but since I started doing it, I became a better hitter by going the other way."

As a player, Stargell practiced what he would later, as a coach, preach. Milt May, a former teammate of his with the Pirates, and himself a hitting coach, said that in batting practice Stargell actually worked on going the other way quite a bit. Perez concurred, "Yeah, that's what he was doing all the time. He'd tell us and we'd watch him." Perez admired the fact that Stargell could work on such a skill and still have the ability to murder balls by pulling them for monumental home runs—"out of the stadium to right field."

However, he pointed out that it's not merely hitting coaches who influence young hitters. "As a manager, there [was] a guy who, I think, is why I'm here in the big leagues, Grady Little. Grady was my manager for five years. He wanted me to play for his teams all the time."

Little not only taught Perez aspects of hitting, he mentored him on "all the stuff. He was a catcher, and he taught me a lot of stuff about catching. I learned a lot from him." It's not uncommon for big leaguers to look back fondly on a coach or manager, giving them credit for success.

Francona said that when it comes to hitting coaches, their advice, and players' responses to coaches, "everybody's different. *Everybody's* different. Everybody has their own philosophy, [but I] just wanted to see the ball and hit the ball. You can talk about your stance, you can talk about balance, you can talk about your stride, but if you don't see the ball, you have no chance."

He was exposed to countless "hitting coaches" in his life: "Everybody, at one point, *thought* they were a coach—even a lot of pitchers who sat the bench. There were some times I was going so bad, I'd listen to the batboy," he joked. "I probably listened to my father more than anybody," he said, referring to former big-leaguer Tito, who once hit .363. Growing up around the major-league backdrop, Terry gained knowledge almost through osmosis. He'd listen to his father talking baseball with teammates and gain insights most kids would never be exposed to.

There were other good influences in his life. "I was around Billy deMars, Terry Crowley—as a player he was already being a hitting instructor—and a lot of [other] good ones."

Francona believes that many differences he encountered among various hitting coaches weren't drastic philosophical variations, but rather dealt with "personalities and how [lessons] are presented. As a hitter, you gotta hit how you hit, and hitting instructors—the really good ones I've seen—they take their hitters and they take their strengths and they work off of that. And the hitters don't adapt to the instructor, the instructor adapts to the hitter." That philosophy is akin to something Dick Williams once said of successful managing: a good leader strives to put his players in situations where they will succeed, not in a spot where they are almost certain to fail.

The June 2002 *Baseball Digest* featured an article on Sammy Sosa. Teddy Greenstein wrote that Sosa's one-time hitting coach, Jeff Pentland, got Sosa to "lower his hands, to utilize his legs as a power source and, most importantly, to eliminate the 'springiness' in his swing." Pentland said, "Sammy always seemed like he was in a hurry to hit the ball." A coach's input is highly beneficial when he not only notices a flaw, however minor, but can then influence and improve the hitter.

Hitting coach pioneer Harry "The Hat" Walker essentially agreed, yet minimized the instructor's importance. He offered, "No batting coach can do anything to make a man a better hitter than he is. He may, once in a while, teach a man to overcome some basic flaw in his technique, a flaw which had been robbing him of the benefits of his natural ability." Walker believed that a coach should observe his hitters and see how they looked and moved when hitting well. Then, when a hitter tailed off, the coach should try to help guide him back on track.

Charlie Manuel said he believes a coach must have leadership qualities. He thought he made a good instructor because "I get along with the players, and I have the respect of the players, and I helped develop a lot of players."

Thome respected Manuel's ability so much that when Thome went to the Phillies in 2003 they hired Manuel as a hitting instructor, some say mainly to please free agent Thome. In his first spring training there, Manuel addressed a problem Thome had experienced for much of his career, a tendency to get off to bad starts. "It's very important that Jimmy keys down at the start of the year and works his way into it," Manuel stated. "Jimmy wants to come out of the gate hitting home runs. If [he] gets a few hits early, he'll be all right. Otherwise, he might press and start over-swinging." It felt good for Thome to have an instructor on the scene who already knew him and his trends very well.

That was also the case with big Frank Thomas. After several off-seasons, a frustrated Thomas contacted his old hitting instructor, Walt Hriniak. His plea for help was perceived by the White Sox front office as a good sign, the first step of a much-needed remedy. Like a person suffering from an addiction finally admitting the need for help, Thomas saw the need for Hriniak to correct a hitting flaw.

Over the off-season months of 1999, Hriniak viewed all of Thomas's hitting tapes from the previous several seasons and discovered two glaring flaws. Then it was time to hit the cage with Thomas. "He had me fixed in 30 minutes," beamed Thomas. After hitting only 15 homers with 77 RBIs in 1999, it must have felt great to take the teachings of Hriniak and break out with a .328 season in 2000, with a booming 43 homers and 143 runs driven in.

However, this was not a long-lasting cure. Thomas was not infallible, not injury immune, and not permanently back to putting up the old Frank Thomas numbers. By 2001 his batting average had fallen to .221, and he managed to play in only 20 games.

In February of 2003 Thomas again worked out with the coach he felt so comfortable with. Hriniak mainly stressed hitting the ball the other way, as Thomas had done so successfully in the past.

Players who make it to the majors and last any length of time are invariably exposed to numerous hitting coaches. If each one has a slightly different philosophy, a player can be inundated with sometimes contradictory advice. Through 2002, twelve-year big-league veteran Bill Haselman estimated he had been instructed by about "six [different hitting coaches], seven maybe. Some guys are more mechanical [in their approach], some guys are more mental. Some guys want you to approach things by just getting the mechanics down; other guys talk about what the pitchers throw and how to approach certain pitches. Those are the two basic different philosophies."

One might expect an occasional dispute or, at the very least, a disagreement to crop up between teacher and pupil. Haselman says that's not so. "Never. Not up here [in the majors] because I think hitting coaches up here do a great job of letting you do what you're supposed to do. I mean, you got here for a reason. And then they just work with that. Rudy [Jaramillo] is outstanding with that. He works with what you have. I think the guys that try to change you are looking for credit or something. I don't know what they're doing, but I've never really had anybody like that as a hitting coach."

He could, however, envision a circumstance in the minors where a coach just might try to make major alterations. "Maybe if a guy comes from high school or college and just has a terrible-looking swing, then that's a whole different thing. That's something that needs to be done, probably." That could occur, Haselman imagined, with a kid who had holes in his swing but got drafted because "maybe he's a defensive wizard or maybe he's fast as can be and they see a lot of potential in him and they think that they can work with him and get him to where they want."

When Ken Griffey Sr. was drafted by the Reds out of Donora, Pennsylvania, he had a ton of raw talent, including blinding speed. A Cincinnati scout felt the organization should pick him, believing Griffey would blossom into a major-league talent. Griffey said, though, that most of the improvement that took place came from within, not from minor-league coaching. He worked out on his own shortly after getting drafted to improve his already blistering speed and soon acquired other skills such as bunting. Before long, he embarked on a 19-year major-league career, hitting an impressive .296 over that span.

A seldom-discussed, almost hidden secret of players' success is consistency throughout the entire organization. Many historians believe that Branch Rickey's Dodgers teams were so successful because he not only had a wide web of minor-league teams, but he had all his minor-league players learning the game "the Dodgers way." Likewise with Texas, Jaramillo expounded, "Butch Wynegar's my minor-league hitting instructor and he's great. He's real loyal to me and I appreciate that, and I know the [other minor-league] coaches and managers are, too. So we do the same things throughout the system, which doesn't happen all the time [in baseball]."

Another seldom-considered aspect of the hitting coach is working with a switch hitter. That, according to Rettenmund, is more difficult than helping the other hitters. "I'm not big on switch hitters," he said, "simply because after so many years they become better hitters from the left side, and they're supposed to keep both sides of the plate sharp [but they don't]. I've been fortunate enough to watch guys like Chipper Jones and Ken Caminiti, and those two guys probably were about the best at both sides of the plate.

"Now, the guy they have in Atlanta, Rafael Furcal, I think he'd lead the league in hitting if he'd only hit right-handed because he's got tre-mendous pop—I don't mean home-run pop, I mean [he's] a hard line-drive hitter—and he can run like heck, and he can use the whole field. You just can't defense him right-handed. Everyone likes him from the left side because he can get his 10 or 15 bunts a year, but in between he hits .240.

"And they've got another kid in Atlanta, Wilson Betemit. He's a super-duper prospect," continued Rettenmund. "What they've done with these kids is they get them when they're 16 or 17 years old and they make them switch hitters. Caminiti and Steve Finley started switch hitting when they were what—three or four or five." He did concede that considering his late start, Furcal, in just a short span of about three years, became "amazing" with the bat, going from nowhere to the majors.

Rettenmund listed J. T. Snow as being typical of a switch hitter who gives it up to go to the left side. "Orlando Merced did too. He was with Houston the last couple of years, and he only hits left-handed now." Merced was a switch hitter from the day he turned professional in the mid-1980s until 1993 when he looked at his .193 average as a righty (more than 150 at-bats against southpaws) and decided a change was badly needed. Batting exclusively as a lefty, over his next 626 at-bats versus lefties he hit 63 points higher than he had before when facing lefties, proving his deci-sion was a wise one. Other players who have dropped their switch-hitting ways in mid-career include Rich Becker and Mariano Duncan, who was on two world champion teams with Cincinnati and the Yankees.

When all is said and done, McGraw believes that the art of hitting is sometimes overanalyzed. While that may sound ironic coming from a hitting coach, he explained, "They make too much of hitting. It's not that hard if you know the basics." Still, maybe Tris Speaker was correct: with so many basics to be explored, explaining successful batting fully seems a nearly impossible task.

12

Intangibles and Other Insights

The Ballparks

ACCORDING TO AN old story, when Babe Ruth walked into Wrigley Field for the 1932 World Series, he glanced around the hitters' park and uttered, "I'd play for half my salary if I could hit in this dump all the time."

Of course, it may have been a case of the outfield grass being greener on the other side, since his own home park was considered to be a great place to hit for left-handers. Decades after Ruth was gone, Kevin Maas was with the Yankees and enjoyed a couple of seasons in which he put up solid (20-plus homers) power numbers. As a lefty, he couldn't help but notice the coziness of the right-field home-run target at Yankee Stadium. He said, "Sometimes when I'm not doing well, the 314 feet down the line comes into play."

He said that at times he might turn on the ball, not get good wood on it, and still see it sail over the wall. "You don't always have to get all of it to hit it out down the line. When I'm hitting well, no park can hold me. If a power hitter hits hard line drives and gets it up in the air, it'll go." With that in mind, he said a goal should be to "put the ball in play. Home runs, from my experience, are accidents," he said.

Kevin Reimer, one of a handful of players to hit a ball over the right-field wall at Camden Yards and onto Eutaw Street, also said that hitters should try to ignore parks' short porches such as Camden's 318 feet down the line in right. "You just try to make good contact, try to stay on it. If you don't, you'll leave the place with bad habits that'll turn into a week-long slump."

Over the years the ballpark in which a hitter plays his home contests (typically between 70 and 80 games per season for the regulars) can be a huge factor. Many experts have speculated as to what would have happened if Ted Williams would have been traded from the Red Sox to the Yankees for Joe DiMaggio. The consensus is that both players would have greatly benefited from their new home parks. DiMaggio, a right-handed hitter, would have zeroed in (and over) the Green Monster in left field at Fenway while Williams would have cracked many balls over the short porch in right at Yankee Stadium.

High-scoring games are nothing unusual in Boston's Fenway Park. Jim Rice, who played there for 16 seasons, said his favorite parks were Yankee Stadium, Tiger Stadium, and Fenway. He reminisced that in Boston "a lot of my line drives were singles, maybe doubles. In any other ball parks, they'd have been outs."

However, Fred Lynn said that it's a misconception to think that Fenway is a great park for right-handed hitters. He said it's "a lefty hitter's park and always will be. A right-handed hitter can't reach the right-field wall in Fenway. It's too deep. But a lefty can turn his swing inside out and hit the close left-field wall. I did that countless times."

A few other older parks notorious for being hitters' parks included Philadelphia's Baker Bowl, known as one of baseball's most famous bandboxes; the "Launching Pad," Fulton County Stadium in Atlanta; and Wrigley Field in Chicago, when the wind is blowing out.

Forbes Field in Pittsburgh was a fine park for line-drive hitters, but not especially so for sluggers. Throughout its long history (1909–1970), nearly 5,000 games were played at the venerable park, yet there was never a no-hitter thrown there. Forbes had a spacious outfield, which helped such hitters as Paul and Lloyd Waner, Honus Wagner, Pie Traynor, and many others all the way up to Matty Alou, Al Oliver, and Roberto Clemente. In fact, the record for the most triples in a single season is a staggering 36 by Pirate Owen Wilson. And on May 30, 1925, the Bucs hit a record five triples in a game.

For much of its existence, the deepest part of the park, which was slightly to left center by the flagpole, was an astronomical 457 feet (at first it was 462 feet) from home plate. In left-center and right-center, a 406-foot-plus poke was required to clear the ivy-clad wall. Such a dimension was fine for peppering doubles and triples, but hardly the distance of an intimate power alley. It was also a remote 365 feet down the left-field line and at times as far as 376 feet down the other line.

Home-run legend Ralph Kiner needed only one glimpse at the generous dimensions of Forbes to comment, "I wanted to telephone the scout who signed me, Hollis Thurston, [and ask] how could he have done this to me?"

Baseball has gone through many cycles. At one time cookie-cutter ballparks prevailed. Further, in one long-ago era, hitting 10 home runs in a year was considered an unusual show of power. In Aaron's day, hitting in the 40 range was great. Now, it almost seems as if a batter has to collect 50 to 70 to be considered a slugger.

Jim Riggleman has been coaching and managing long enough to see such changes and says, "I think hitters have just gotten better. They've kind of become immune to what pitchers have to offer. There's been no pitch that's come along to set them back the way the forkball did years ago, the slider did 25 years ago. Pitchers are going to have to come up with something, or we're going to have to raise the mound, because the hitters are just getting bigger and stronger and the ballparks are getting smaller."

Whether hitters today are better than the Ruths and Aarons is debatable. However, small parks are probably more significant than many fans might imagine. Today a large number of parks either have bandbox dimensions (e.g., Minute Maid Park in Houston, especially cozy and inviting down the left-field line) or are clearly hitter friendly (Denver's Coors Field comes to mind).

Matt Lawton joined the Cleveland Indians in 2002, and he couldn't have been more delighted, since Jacobs Field had "always been one of my favorite parks. I love hitting here; this was always my favorite."

In the meantime, Ellis Burks, who put up huge numbers when he played for Colorado at mile-high Coors Field, confirmed what everyone knew—that playing there clearly is an advantage for hitters. "It's probably going to add ten points on your average per year, and I'd say you're probably going to get an extra four, five homers."

In May 2000 Helton told *USA Today/Baseball Weekly* that he readily admits he absolutely benefits from hitting at Coors. He not only feels comfortable hitting there, but he also likes and benefits from the park's huge outfield, which leads to "a lot of broken-bat hits. The outfielders play so deep, they can't get to them. The pitcher gets frustrated and gets too fine because he doesn't want to throw anything down the middle of the plate. Then he starts walking guys, and you have huge innings."

Another Rockies hitter, Jay Payton, said Coors was his favorite park because not only is it a wide-open park for balls to fall in, but hitters see the ball well there and the ball tends to carry well. Of course that was also true of the Rockies' first home park, Mile-High Stadium. When Lance Parrish saw how well the ball soared there, he commented, "I think the word got around that all you really wanted to do was to get the ball in the air there." However, on the debit side, he also said that he felt that many hitters messed up their swing at Coors Field by trying for the fences.

When Bonds was asked in August 2002 how well he thought his career would have gone had he stayed in a Pirates uniform and played at PNC Park, he replied, "This park is a joke. The ball just flies out of here. I don't even want to know how many more home runs I would have if I would have played here for seven years [instead of the seven seasons he spent in San Francisco's not-so-hitter-friendly Candlestick Park]."

Conversely, Detroit Tigers slugger Bobby Higginson, who plays his home games in Comerica Park, was, no doubt, robbed of many home runs because of that park's deep dimensions. He observed that the park "plays pretty big. We call it Comerica National Park." By 2003 Tigers officials complied with their hitters' requests and reduced the distance from home plate to the wall in left-center from 395 feet to 370. Former Tiger Robert Fick liked the change. He believes that one reason Juan Gonzalez only spent one season as a Tiger was because of the deep dimensions of the park.

When a new ballpark is unveiled, one of the first things that hitters do is check out the park's home-run factors. Not only are its dimensions considered, but also wind tendencies, atmospheric conditions (Does the ball carry well? Will it go farther when the temperature heats up?), and so on. When Seattle's SAFECO Field first opened in July of 1999, fans of power hitters such as Ken Griffey Jr. were alarmed to note that home-run totals were diminishing. Accustomed to the Kingdome, where homers had flown with ease, Seattle hitters accumulated only 47 home runs from mid-July through the end of that season at home.

However, not everyone is home-run crazy. Lawton said he doesn't think too much about the park he plays in on a given day. "You just go out and play," he said. "I play in a bandbox everyday. You can't get carried away with it. You just got to go up there and try to play your game." He said that approach works for him, as, not being a power hitter, he doesn't want to "get caught up in hitting home runs."

With that in mind, he doesn't try to step up his power at all even if, say, the wind is blowing out briskly. "It doesn't change my game." Surprisingly, when the wind conditions are the opposite, Lawton said that somehow those are the days he hits some of his best shots. "When the wind is blowing in like 100 miles an hour, I usually tear into one that day. That's just how it happens. Any other day it probably would've been a homer."

Robby Thompson realizes that a hitter with at least a modicum of power can be tempted by hitting in a snug ballpark. In an effort to boost his home runs, he may further be seduced to change his approach to the game. However, Thompson feels that is a mistake. "I think you have to basically take the same approach. You can't go out there thinking, 'It's a small ballpark; I'm going to hit two, three balls out of the ballpark today.' You go up with the same approach—try to hit hard line drives. If you get underneath it a little bit, you get the carry. Home runs are hit, [but] believe me, guys aren't going up there trying to hit a home run. Most of the time those are accidents."

Like Lawton, Thompson doesn't advise changing a basic hitting approach even if, say, during pregame work he notices the wind is blowing in hard. "That wind may switch by the time we get out there," he said.

"[Use] the same approach. Try to get the ball on a line. [Hit] hard ground balls, line drives."

Still, many hitters do take into consideration a ballpark's factors such as the weather or field conditions. One slugger said that the first thing he'd look at after walking up the dugout steps and onto the field was the flag. A head wind of 10 miles per hour at Wrigley Field, for example, will take a ball that would normally travel 400 feet for a home run and hold it down to a 370-foot routine out. An adjustment in his intentions at the plate may result. Likewise, on a muddy, wet, or slow field, laying down a bunt doesn't make sense.

Busch Stadium in St. Louis seems to have a split personality. For years it was unkind to power hitters. Manager Whitey Herzog utilized his speedy hitters there, urging them to make contact and take off running. The greyhounds often hit the ball into the alleys and scampered for extra bases, but home-run hitters languished there. Hitters such as Jack Clark led the Cardinals in homers, usually with totals in the vicinity of 30, rather than 40 or more. When Busch was remodeled, it became more conducive to the power game. Mark McGwire lit the stadium up for home-run totals of 70 in 1998 and 65 in 1999.

Joe Torre liked hitting in Busch Stadium during his Cardinals days. "Playing there helped me because basically I was a line-drive hitter, and the gaps were wide—and I think it helped me a great deal." While fans normally think a turf surface helps speedy hitters, the quick playing surface of the Busch infield aided Torre, a slow runner. "I hit a lot of balls on the ground. Hell, I led the league in double plays for a couple, three years in a row," he admitted. Then he detailed how many of the balls he hit hard scooted through the infield holes.

Yet another home-field advantage is the cheating some grounds crews do for their team. Many teams have their crews tailor the field for their hitters. The crew might pound down or bake the dirt around home plate if their team tends to hit a lot of choppers. For a team with fine bunters, the foul lines can be built up or sloped slightly, allowing (almost forcing) bunts to stay in fair territory. Grass can be cut extremely short or allowed to grow thick and lush depending upon the type of hitters and defense a team has.

Teams have even been known to help their offense by using two sets of baseballs: a set of regulation balls and a set stored in freezers the night before to deaden them.

Colorful team owner Bill Veeck actually moved his fences in or out prior to a series, depending upon the strengths of his club and those of the opponents. If a powerful club was coming to town, Veeck would, cheerleader-like, exhort his grounds crew to, "Push 'em back, waaay back." If Veeck's team could outslug a team, the fences moved in, nestling as near the infield as Veeck dared to order. He did so, of course, under the darkness of night, fully aware that what he was doing was illegal.

According to *Take Me Out to the Ballpark* by Josh Leventhal, the groundskeepers for the Tigers would soak the area in front of home plate to benefit Cobb. His bunts tended to stay fair due to the soggy conditions there.

Elsewhere, some crews tailor the pitcher's mound to suit their staff or to thwart an opposing pitcher, and thereby help their own hitters. Leventhal wrote, "Hall of Fame pitcher Catfish Hunter, for example, preferred a soft mound; opposing groundskeepers would pack it down or water it and let the sun harden it before a game." And, of course, some parks purposely create visitor's bullpen mounds so that they vary from the one on the field. That way, pitchers warming up don't get used to the conditions they'll face in the game.

Rickey Henderson said he could recall several players who, like Matty Alou in Forbes Field, benefited from a figurative home-court advantage. "[Jose] Cruz and Harold Reynolds in Seattle used the turf to [their] advantage." He could have thrown in names such as Willie Wilson, Omar Moreno, and, lately, the Twins' crew of hitters (Cristian Guzman, et al.) who delight in hitting on the quick surface in the Metrodome. However, Henderson believes that ballparks' influence isn't as big a factor as it used to be. He said one doesn't see too many hitters nowadays gaining a big advantage as Punch-and-Judy hitter Alou did, because "everybody's trying to hit the home run; they ain't trying to slap hit."

However, David Eckstein says the Angels get a kick from the booming sound of the fans' Thunderstix. "I love playing with a lot of noise," he said. "It might hurt your ears, but it's a good thing." The same held true at times for Twins players in the Metrodome, especially during postseason play. In fact, most players say they are aware of the noise and admit they do get pumped up by the home crowd's cheering.

There are so many new ballparks now that hitters are going about their craft under nearly ideal conditions. For example, lighting for night games is vastly improved over what it used to be. Even so, said Picciolo, "I think the majority of hitters probably [still] prefer day baseball. It can wear you out [the heat of day contests], as evidenced in Chicago [Wrigley Field still hosts numerous day games], but I know a lot of them like the day games and like hitting in daylight." He believes that natural sunlight is probably more conducive to hitting than even the most modern artificial lighting of any facility.

Biggio compared modern lighting with natural daylight, starting with a park famous for its day baseball. "Actually, at Wrigley, you see the ball pretty good at nighttime there, but you don't see it as well on the field [on defense]."

At times, though, he said a day game can actually have too much light. "Sometimes it's brighter and it's hard. It isn't that easy seeing that ball sometimes for a day game at Wrigley, coming out of those people." He said there is no cut-and-dried answer as far as which way he'd rather hit. He even indicated that he has no idea if he hits for a better average during day contests, "and I don't really care," he laughed. Lighting aside, he said, "I'd much rather play a night game. "You can sleep in, in the morning. A day game, you're not as strong; night games you're stronger—you get your rest."

Picciolo commented, "The tough time is when you have these starts at five o'clock, or you have these five-fifteen, five-thirty starts when the shadows are over home plate. The first three or four innings, a definite advantage goes to the pitcher." Under those conditions, a batter watches a ball leave the pitcher's hand while gazing out at the mound, which is sun-baked, but through the shade of where he is standing at the plate. It is extremely difficult for a hitter to follow the path of a ball as it sizzles through such diverse lighting conditions.

Russell Branyan added, "Lighting has a lot to do with how you hit and the backdrop. Boston's [Fenway Park] is pretty tough. It's an old ballpark. I was talking to one of my old coaches, and he said when he played at Fenway on Sundays everybody would come in from church and everybody would be wearing white shirts and it was always a 2-1, 1-0 ball game on Sundays back then. Really low-scoring games, but that was all part of baseball back then. Now they really focus on getting a good backdrop, a good hitting background, and good lighting. It's really offensive oriented, but when you go into a new ballpark, you've really gotta check things out."

More than a few hitters who've been hit by pitches have admitted that they never saw the ball well or never saw it at all. Even fielders have had problems. Odell Hale, a third baseman, once lost a ball amidst a background of white shirts. It ricocheted off his head and into the hands of the shortstop who wound up turning a triple play.

Nowadays, the colors of the hitters' backdrops have usually been studied thoroughly. Brent Butler said that hitters don't exactly look at results of such studies, but they do tend to like a dark hitting backdrop, and black and green work quite well. With all that in mind, new ballparks provide great hitting backgrounds, especially when contrasted to conditions that existed decades ago at the major-league level.

Sexson agreed that the background matters a great deal for hitters. "The backdrop's the main part of the field. The main thing as a hitter is you want to be able to see the ball. For the most part, that's how you're going to best be able to hit the ball, by *seeing* it. All the new ballparks now are really good with the exception of Cincinnati [the year they were] going through a transitional stage." He was referring to the year the park there, Cinergy Field, was partly dismantled in preparation for the opening of Great American Ball Park. Even then, he said the backdrop in Cincy was "OK, but it could [have been] better."

Branyan commented, "Most of them [big-league ballparks' hitting backgrounds] are pretty good nowadays; minor-league fields are what's tough. They have all the signs, the endorsements [plastered all over the center-field walls]."

Even the older parks have improved, according to Sexson, who said, "Fenway has the black tarp covering up the seats there. And the Green Monster, obviously, goes all the way out into center, so you can see the ball good there, too. Obviously you don't want it [the backdrop] to be light;

you want it to be as dark as possible [and they now are]." In some parks, hitters are looking into a sea of deep-green ivy, as is the case at Baltimore's Camden Yards.

On the other hand, Lawton singled out two newer parks that perhaps should have put more study into helping hitters' vision. "Seattle has a tough backdrop, especially [during] day games, and Detroit [does too]. If you play there during the day, the first couple at-bats is like giving it away because you can't see the ball." He said at Comerica the problems are with the lighting and "a lot of shadows. The sun reflects off of this and that so it gets to be a little difficult sometimes."

Touching again on how heat can wilt hitters, Sosa concurred with Picciolo. When the Cubs wanted permission to play 30 to 40 night games, up from the 18 per season they were permitted when they first installed lights in 1988, Sosa spoke up. "It will give us a better chance to win." He said players need the night contests in order to "have more energy." Rangers fans could relate to that, since they felt their team often tended to fade down the stretch due to the intense Texas sun.

When it comes to a home-field advantage for hitters, few people consider the official scorer. On a hit-versus-error call that could go either way, it never hurts to play in a city with a friendly, generous official scorer. For years St. Louis Cardinals hitters seemed to benefit more than most teams' players due to a scorekeeper who awarded Cardinals batters hits on numerous close decisions.

Some players go so far as to argue with the scorer in an attempt to improve their batting averages. Robby Alomar is said to have convinced scorers to reverse some rulings, giving Alomar a hit after initially charging an error on the other team's defense. In fact, several fiery players have actually called up to the press box from the dugout phone to ask, beg, or demand favorable decisions from scorekeepers during games.

Experience

One intangible that a player can't rush is experience. Normally, rookies don't come onto the scene, do well from the start, and sail through a long career with few downfalls.

Fryman said that virtually all young players have to pay some dues. He believed that he played with intensity from his rookie year on. However, he stated, "What takes time is to learn how to have that constant approach, how to put the ups and downs behind you, and not ride your emotions so much as a young player or any young person does. They're very controlled by their emotions. As an old player you learn how to even those things out a little bit."

Older players also get to know various pitchers so well, it's as if they develop a baseball extrasensory perception. During his stellar 1971 season, Joe Torre said he felt as if he knew what pitches were coming—he had studied pitchers' tendencies that well. "I remember there was one game we were playing in Montreal, and John Strohmayer was their pitcher. I told Bob Gibson on the way to the ballpark, 'I'm going to hit a high slider out of the park off him.'

"Well, the first time up he threw me a slider for a strike low and away, another slider for a strike low and away, and a curveball—strike three. I took three pitches, and I very rarely did that. I didn't even know he threw a curveball," he confessed.

"Next time up, I looked for a slider again, and he threw me a fastball. I hit a single up the middle.

"Third time up, I had two men on base and he threw me a high slider. I hit a home run. I mean that's the kind of concentration and patience you've got to have to be a good hitter." Naturally, all that comes with age and big-league experience.

Juan Gonzalez has always been a big run producer. For half of the 1998 season, he found himself on a pace to break Hack Wilson's seemingly insurmountable single-season RBI mark of 191. By that year's All-Star break on July 5, he had reached the 100-RBI plateau (with 101, just two shy of the midseason record) and ended with a league-leading 157 RBIs. He attributed his success to his focus, saying he concentrated better when men were on base.

During Gregg Jefferies's latter years in the majors, he said his pregame preparation wasn't as intense as it had been in his early days in the majors, but that came about simply because his experience helped him compensate. His main method of getting ready to face a pitcher was not much more complex than watching videos. He took a fundamental approach, thinking about the pitcher he was to face. Thanks to video, it was an easy task for him. "That's pretty much it. I mean, being in the league for so long, you're a lot more relaxed. When I face a guy, I just think about how he got me out and what he wants to throw."

One year after Yankee Danny Tartabull enjoyed a burst of power, he said he noticed that teams were pitching him differently. "I'm pretty much a free swinger," he said. "But I'm on a 100-walk pace, and that's very unusual for me." Due to experience, he said he had "learned to be more patient and mature in certain situations, to take what they're giving me."

Another former Yankee, Clete Boyer, looked at a young Robin Ventura and guessed he'd never be a 40-home-run-a-year hitter but said, "I see him as being around 20 a year, and, when you get older, you learn to pull more, and you get stronger." Back then, Boyer thought Ventura was "just trying to make contact." Ventura did learn his lessons well and even broke out with a couple of 30-plus-home-run seasons.

According to most observers, a hitter will reach his prime somewhere in his late 20s or early 30s. For example, the average age of a major-league batting champ is 28. Experts feel that it takes a hitter about 1,500 at-bats in the minors alone before he's ready to face big-league pitching. When his son made it to the majors after a paltry 462 minor-league at-bats, Ken Griffey Sr. was genuinely surprised, but pleased.

The majority of rookies and young players don't do well at first. They have to feel their way. Then there are those who do well the first time through the league, only to find the pitchers have figured them out a little later in the year. Likewise, some players manage to put together a nice rookie season but find pitchers making adjustments to them by their second year. The result is known as the sophomore jinx. Of course, many young hitters don't make it at all, lasting for only a brief time at the big-league level.

Finally, there are those young hitters who seemed to be ready for the majors but get sent back to the minors for more seasoning, and who are able to climb back to the majors and finally succeed. In 2002 players such as the highly touted Sean Burroughs and Hank Blalock proved that there's no such thing as a sure thing. Blalock lasted only a short time with the Rangers before they shipped him back to the minors. Burroughs spent part of the year on the disabled list and was also sent down. Just as it takes time to learn who will make it and who won't, it takes experience to make a player complete. Both Burroughs and Blalock rebounded with impressive major-league seasons in 2003, with Blalock hitting the game-winning home run in the All-Star game.

Health

Cliff Floyd of the New York Mets gave his opinion of what building blocks it would take to assemble the ideal ballplayer. He listed physical attributes including Barry Bonds's wrists and Vladimir Guerrero's arms before adding an intangible: Cal Ripken's health. A hitter simply can't put up numbers if he's not healthy and in the lineup regularly.

When Fred McGriff, known as "Crime Dog," went on the disabled list in 2003, he reflected, "I pride myself on going out there every day and staying away from injuries, but this time, it got me." Players like McGriff, who didn't go on the disabled list until his 18th big-league season, are indeed rare. Iron men such as Lou Gehrig and Cal Ripken Jr. are essentially extinct today. Ripken not only didn't miss contests, he seldom even missed innings.

For most mortal hitters, a breather now and then is vital, in order to recharge one's batteries during the scorching days of summer. However, most players agree that there are times when a player must play with nagging injuries or fatigue and somehow manage to overcome those obstacles. Asking out of the lineup when not at 100 percent health or when a tough pitcher is on the mound is not a respected trait for ballplayers, but some choose to beg off to protect their stats.

No one knows the entire truth except David Justice, but he was accused of asking out of the lineup when he should have sucked it up and played in the fifth game of the 1999 Division Series. A *Cleveland Plain Dealer* article was scathing. "In a win-or-go-home situation," the paper reported, "he chose to go home, taking the night off because of a stiff neck."

Pitcher Justin Speier said, "You see guys that go out there, real professional about it. They go out there and play with little, nagging injuries—no one's ever 100 percent. Guys who play through that show us younger guys that, 'Hey, you go out there and you play through aches and pains.' My dad [major-league shortstop Chris] played at 100 percent maybe three times in his whole career, and he played 19 years. That's just one of those things—you're never going to be 100 percent."

Many cases of players begging off don't even get publicized. It was not at all uncommon for players, especially left-handed hitters, to ask for a day off when facing, say, Randy Johnson or a young Vida Blue. Some players say not playing beats taking an unproductive (to both the hitter and his team) "oh-fer."

When John Kruk faced Johnson in an All-Star game, he, almost comically, bailed out—almost scampering entirely out of the box. Larry Walker, in mock fear of Johnson, turned his batting helmet around and faced the "Big Unit" while batting righty instead of his normal lefty. Even established veterans have admitted an aversion to facing wild or extremely fast young pitchers, such as Bob Feller or Sandy Koufax. One batter argued a called strike thrown by Walter Johnson. The overwhelmed hitter contended that the pitch "sounded high to me."

In its proper place, there is nothing wrong with seeking a little rest. Aging stars are typically rested on a day game following a night game. In addition, even younger players are given a day or two off at times. During the draining days down the stretch it certainly pays to keep hitters fresh, as a fatigued hitter is rarely, if ever, a productive one.

In 2002 Biggio, then 36 years old, went through a stretch of playing 10 games, with 6 of the contests being afternoon affairs. "When you mix day games in with night games, it's tough to bounce back," Biggio said. "When you get into August and September, these are the dog days."

Joe Morgan said Sparky Anderson was careful not to overuse his established, older stars such as Tony Perez and especially Johnny Bench, giving him a day off from his grueling catching duties. Some managers will rest such hitters by playing them at a less demanding defensive post or, in the American League, by making them the DH.

Die-hard players say as long as they're not in traction, they want to take to the field. Eddie Murray never wanted to sit. "I went out and played. The first time I missed a game, I was mad at [his Orioles manager] Earl [Weaver]. By the end of the third inning, I was in there. That was me. I didn't come to sit down; I came to work."

Brent Butler said such determination and dedication are important. "We have a bunch of gamers on our team [the Rockies]," he said. "I know there are a lot of guys who don't feel good, but they go out there everyday and they give everything they have."

It's obvious that during a long season it's impossible to stay 100 percent healthy. Relief pitcher Scott Stewart of the Expos said that the aches and pains his arm endures in spring training basically stay with him all year long. Hitters, likewise, can have their performance diminished by injuries.

Rettenmund may have surprised some people when he asserted, "Jose Canseco was potentially the best all-around player I've ever seen, but he just never got there. He had injuries, and [because of them] it didn't pan out for him."

Some fans consider big leaguers to be spoiled. They might not realize or understand that a nagging "little" injury can cost a hitter many points off his batting average or force him out of the lineup. Those fans are fond of saying, "His injury wouldn't keep me from working the assembly line." They're correct to a point, but the job of a major-league hitter is a very specialized one.

If a player doesn't complain to the media about his injury, some fans may think that the hitter is a stiff, a bum, or over the hill, and that's simply not always the case. For instance, Tom Lampkin noted, "Thumbs can definitely [mess up a hitter's swing] because that's what you're holding on to the bat with. There are other injuries that guys have just on a daily basis, little aches and pains that sometimes hamper you, but hands, especially when it comes to hitting, is something a little bit different. You know, some guys play with it better than others, and some guys are able to get through it where other guys can't. Nobody really knows the severity of injuries until you actually have them yourself. So it's hard to point fingers at anybody that has an injury because nobody really knows what it feels like." Often when a troublesome injury heals, pitchers and the fickle fans realize the hitter can still be productive.

Lampkin mentioned two other injuries that can cause a player's offensive game to take a swan-dive. "A lot of guys have sore muscles in the rib cage, which really hampers you when you swing, when you twist, and when you start and when you finish." He continued, "Elbows—a lot of times when guys swing and they hyperextend that elbow, that's something that guys struggle with because they don't really want to let the whole thing go because they're afraid to get out in front and miss the ball and do some more damage."

Plus, to compensate for their elbow pain, a hitter might "let the ball come even deeper, so maybe not to let them get fooled on as many pitches, because usually when you snap is when you think something's coming, and all of a sudden it slows down or falls away and you end up being way out in front of it."

So, instead of waiting on the ball, which hitters want to do, a bad swing is the result. "You ultimately want to let the ball get in on you," he continued, "but you want to be able to have confidence in your swing that you can go ahead and let it go and not have to worry about your elbow."

In this regard, today's players have an advantage over hitters from the early days of the game. For example, when Bagwell sustained hand injuries, he was able to return to the game wearing a velcro-attached pad to protect the hand from further harm. Not having to worry about or favor his hand was a plus.

Lampkin said that the most fundamental key to hitting long ago and today is simple: "You can't be afraid to get hit." While that may sound too elementary, he said, "I know some guys who are [afraid]." In fact, the majority of players do jump back in the box after getting hit by a pitch, or, for that matter, after any type of injury. Lampkin continued, "When you do [get hit or hurt], you come in, you get your treatment done, and you see if you can play around it. That's the way I've always been; if you got to tape it, you tape it to provide a little extra support. If you got to put a guard over it, you put a guard over it.

"If you surveyed everybody in this room and everybody in that [opposing] clubhouse, I bet you wouldn't find too many guys who are playing without some type of nagging injury. You learn to play around that. You learn to block it out."

Intimidation

For years now, since the era of Ruth, there has been a correlation between size, power, and intimidation. Ruth may not have possessed the build of a Barry Bonds, but pitchers knew his home-run stroke could send them to a sudden sudsy shower. Cincinnati's Ted Kluszewksi had massive arms and liked to show them off. It seemed as if he warmed up in the on-deck circle by swinging a forest's worth of bats instead of one or two as many players of his era did. "Klu" wore a sleeveless shirt under his vest-like Reds jersey, the better to display his bulging biceps. The art or gift of being able to intimidate pitchers is an intangible that many batters benefit from.

Once a hitter establishes himself as an intimidating force, several perks come to him. Umpires tend to give the superstars close calls. Furthermore, some pitchers may come to fear those batters and work them too carefully, perhaps even grooving a pitch due to their nervousness.

Charles Nagy essentially admitted that pitchers, more so young ones than veterans, can be awed by certain hitters. The 6' 6" Dave Winfield was his selection as the most physically intimidating opponent. "He's just an awesome presence in the box, with his size. Winfield's just an impressive person—his name, his size, and the way he carries himself."

Lee Smith knows that certain hitters can be intimidating, but added his theory. "I think size has a lot to do with it. I don't think a small guy can intimidate you unless you take a guy like Brett Butler. If you've got a guy on third with one out, Butler can do so many things. You've got to watch for the bunt or for him to slap the ball past you."

Jefferies furthered Smith's point. "You're not going to find a little guy that's real intimidating, but you can get respect around the league by being a good guy with men in scoring position—like Keith Hernandez was. A lot of people didn't want to face him with men in scoring position. They'd rather pitch to Darryl Strawberry, who is very intimidating. Figure that one out!

"When you're just talking about pure intimidation," Jefferies continued, "a guy you're in awe of, that's the big strong guy who can hit a ball upper deck. But, talk about a guy who pitchers *worry* about—that's the guy who really gets the runs in." There can be a difference between being intimidating and being a serious threat to pitchers. "Barry Bonds does both. [He's] number one, the one who really stands out. He's the guy who can hurt you—do so many things against you. Guys like him, Ken Griffey, and Frank Thomas. Thomas is the kind of guy who can just do whatever he wants. Those guys are a special breed."

Frank Howard was a really big and intimidating man. He was 6′ 7″ and punished the scales at 255 pounds. Once he hit a pitch that Dick Bosman said he'd never forget. "When Hondo hit 10 home runs in six games in 1968, the last one was off Mickey Lolich," Bosman recalled. "He tried to sneak a fastball past him. Frank top-handed that ball. It had top-spin on it and was kinda' hooking—you hit it hard when it does that. It hit the roof [at Tiger Stadium] and boink—gone."

The muscular Canseco was Joe Carter's pick for a man who personified physical intimidation. "You gotta look at him. I mean he's the guy in my era where he's a legitimate threat every single time to the plate to hit it out."

Cecil Fielder was huge, too. Longtime Detroit announcer Ernie Harwell said with awe, "I think Fielder hits the longest homers. I don't see anybody day in and day out who hits [the ball] as hard as he does." And former Tigers teammate, Lance Parrish, commented, "Fielder and your other big guys are the ones who hit the moon shots."

However, according to longtime St. Louis Cardinals player and manager Red Schoendienst, "A hitter doesn't have to be a big guy to intimidate. Stan Musial was a good hitter, and he could hit the ball out of the ballpark. A lot of guys were like that—they weren't that big in stature, but they had good bat speed—that's the key." He cited three sluggers who fit that bill: the 6-foot Aaron; Mathews, listed at 6′ 1″; and Mays, at 5′ 10½″.

Sparky Anderson said wisely, "It all revolves around fast hands. Aaron and [Ernie] Banks had fast hands, and they didn't have great [tape measure] power. I don't think I ever saw Henry hit the ball a long distance."

Cito Gaston goes along with that thinking. "Aaron was intimidating because if you threw it up there, he was going to hit you somewhere. It doesn't matter how big you are. So, as far as being worried about somebody going to hit a rope off you, to me the two best hitters I saw when I came into the league were certainly Aaron along with Billy Williams, and they're not big people."

Andre Dawson contributed the name of Mike Schmidt to this list. "He just had that awe about him, especially when you fell behind on him. The ball would jump off his bat and carry real well. And he was a good cripple hitter, a good mistake hitter. He was one guy you'd really hate to face, especially with men on base."

Of course the same could be said of Andre Dawson. Joe Carter said with deep respect, "He's another guy you hate to see come to the plate—he's intimidating. He's got that wiry body, but he's strong and he's got some tremendous bat speed."

Another tough out was Yankees captain Thurman Munson, with his intimidating grubby look. Sparky Lyle once said of Munson and his demeanor, "He's not moody, he's just mean. When you're moody, you're nice sometimes."

Rollie Fingers had this take on Minnesota slugger Harmon Killebrew: "It didn't make any difference what I threw—he hit it. And it just wasn't that he hit it, it was where he hit it. If he had accumulated frequent-flyer miles on fly balls off me, he could have gone to Europe and back at least four times."

Parrish called the places that "Killer" deposited balls "unbelievable. We didn't even have guys on our team who could hit close to [where he did] in batting practice. He hit 'em way up there. Oh, man."

Lineups and Teammates

Although it's something a batter can't control, it is a definite plus if he is surrounded by talent in the lineup, or at least has someone hitting behind him in the order to protect him—so pitchers can't work around him and walk him semi-intentionally.

Danny Tartabull put the importance of having protection in the lineup succinctly. "I think it's important to have other power hitters around you, to protect you. It allows you to be in a position to hurt a pitcher [when] they can't work around you."

He was, of course, correct—just ask Barry Bonds. In the 2002 World Series, the Angels, determined to pitch around Bonds, walked him—even with a runner on first, as opposed to employing the traditional strategy of walking him only with first base open. Benito Santiago, batting behind Bonds, offered him no protection. Overall, he hit .231, all of his hits coming on singles. Twelve times he batted right after a walk to Bonds; in nine of those times he came up short, unable to hit the ball out of the infield, including three times when he hit into double plays.

The best teammate duo ever for producing homers was Aaron and Mathews. They played together as Braves from 1954 through 1966, combining for 863 homers to break the former record held by Babe Ruth and Lou Gehrig. Plus, they batted back-to-back in the Braves' lineup.

By way of contrast, in 2002 when Bonds broke the season records for walks drawn and intentional walks, he never had anyone hit behind him to compare with a Mathews. While he and Jeff Kent hit back-to-back, it was Bonds who hit behind Kent for the most part, not the other way around. Kent moved to the number three spot in the order ahead of Bonds on June 27, 2002, and went on a tear the rest of the year, helping the Giants win the NL Wild Card berth in the postseason. As good as Kent was, pitchers chose to pitch to him rather than walk him and have to face Bonds with a man on base.

Dick Miller told a story to *The Sporting News* about Ruth requesting a change in the Yankees' batting order. When Tony Lazzeri was hitting behind Ruth, pitchers issued around 150 walks each year to the Bambino. Finally, when Joe McCarthy became the Yankees' manager, Ruth walked over to him and said, "I'll tell you how to make out the lineup. I'm going to bat third and I want Gehrig behind me. You can fill in the other seven spots." Reportedly McCarthy replied, "That's fine with me, Babe."

For a large chunk of the 2002 season, Sexson, a cleanup hitter, suffered through a prolonged skid in his productivity due to his having little protection around him in the Milwaukee lineup. He had been fine earlier, coming off an excellent first half of the season (19 homers, 62 RBIs), but when those hitting around him began to present little threat to pitchers, Sexson noticed that he wasn't getting as many good pitches to hit. "It's getting tougher," he said. "They seem to be throwing three miles per hour harder to me than the first three guys." Without much help surrounding Sexson in the lineup, and with pitchers working him differently, he hit only seven homers with just 24 runs driven in from the midway point in the season through August 18.

Some players become better, or worse, hitters depending upon where they hit in the order. When the Indians lost some firepower in their lineup at one point, they wanted Manny Ramirez to step it up and hit cleanup. However, he declined, saying he felt he hit better in other spots in the batting order. Conversely, in 2002 Florida manager Jeff Torborg felt Juan Encarnacion was a good enough hitter to man the number-three spot in the order. However, in the sixth slot he had reeled off a 16-for-41 streak.

"I tried moving him up [to third], but he's much more effective down there," explained Torborg. "It seems like hitting in the six hole he's stayed in the groove, so I haven't messed with it."

Some hitters aren't the patient type, and therefore would not do well as a traditional leadoff hitter. Other hitters have even been known to choke when moved to a slot in the order where they were expected to produce big numbers.

Umpires

When a hitter proves himself over the years, he begins to get respect and close calls from umpires. Some batters are quite skilled at "working an umpire," that is, knowing what to say to umpires, how to say it, and even which ones to say something to and which ones to avoid.

Cleveland announcer Matt Underwood argued that players who seldom whine to umps may later reap rewards. He said he believes that when those kinds of hitters do complain, say on a ball-strike call, it actually causes an umpire to think, "I blew that one." Thinking that way may indeed lead the ump to give the batter a make-up call—often during that same at-bat. "You can't tell me that doesn't make a difference," Underwood said. By way of contrast, he pointed out how Paul O'Neill constantly argues, seemingly on every pitch, as if in his mind "no one has ever thrown a strike to him."

He also said, "[Kenny] Lofton has a reputation for arguing, but there's a fine line between letting the ump know you're not happy and complaining too much."

David Justice got away with murder when it came to his check-swing routine. He does have quick hands and is strong enough to keep the bat back, out of the strike zone at times, but sometimes his reputation of holding back and the way he suspends his bat in midair while not out over the plate seems to influence umpires. Underwood simply said, "He does get away with a lot of check swings. He seems to get the benefit of the doubt on a lot of those calls."

Until recent years, umpires either worked their entire career in the National League or in the American League. The only times batters had to adjust to unfamiliar umpires were with rookie umps, in spring training, at the All-Star game, and at the World Series. Hitters realize how important it is to know a given umpire's tendencies, so they study them the way they scrutinize enemy pitchers. Further, for decades experts felt there was a difference in the style of calling balls and strikes between the two leagues.

Matt Lawton spoke of a new wrinkle in the umpiring. "Usually with the umpires, it's like with a pitcher—you get used to their style, how they call the game, but now it's a little bit different because all the umpires are merging. You see a National League guy back there [behind the plate] and you say, 'OK, the plate's going to be wide because he's a National League umpire.' But it doesn't so much mean the same thing now because they've watched the American League guys call the games and vice versa. It's kinda' tough; you just have to see how the game goes on that day." That said, he did indicate that he feels it's getting easier on hitters as the two styles of calling games are starting to come together. All umps have slight variations in their game, though, so learning all one can about individual umpire's styles and tendencies still pays off.

"National League umpires used to call a wider strike zone. Now I don't think that's pretty much the case anymore," Lawton said. "It's just depends on who's pitching on that given day."

What pitches are called for strikes and which are balls can sometimes be influenced by the status of the man on the mound. Superstars still get the close calls. A Greg Maddux gets the benefit of the doubt on borderline pitches, and the border is a lot wider for a star than for a marginal pitcher or rookie. So, it becomes a case of batters having to know how much the zone will stretch when facing various star pitchers.

Lawton asserted that a pitcher such as Pedro Martinez is going to have a "little bigger" strike zone "or if you're playing the Yankees and you're in Yankee Stadium, you know you better be swinging the bat because their pitchers are going to get a wider strike zone." Just ask Dale Mitchell, the final victim in Don Larsen's perfect game during the 1956 World Series. The last pitch, a called strike, was way outside, and one gets the feeling that even if it had been a few inches wider, it would still have been called for a strike.

Lawton said that such conditions are like an unwritten rule. "You know what it's going to be like before the day starts, so you better go up there ready to swing because if you take that day, you're going to be walking back to the dugout a lot. When you see certain guys back there, you know you need to [get in the] batter's box ready to swing." Therefore, he continued, hitters do think about the umps, "especially on day games when they have flights to catch—all those things factor in. You just know how the game's going to be played that day."

Other Factors

Sometimes hitters will ask the umpire to inspect a ball. If the ball has a smudge, making it hard on the batter's vision as the ball comes up to the plate, the ump will throw the ball out of play. A rookie might not think to ask for such an inspection. In the early days of baseball it was common for one or two baseballs to last the entire game; back then, this simple tip wasn't available for a hitter. Likewise, if a hitter suspects a pitcher is doctoring the ball, he can ask that a new, bright, shiny ball be put in play.

Speed is another intangible, one that can be improved somewhat, but basically a player either has it or he doesn't. And those who do are able to reap the benefits with infield hits, close calls at the bag, and bunt hits, giving them an advantage over slower players.

Based on a 500-at-bat season, each hit gained or lost (say, a leg hit in which the batter beats the throw by a half step), is worth two points on his final average. So, a speedy runner may earn, say, 15 hits on close plays at first. With those additional hits, he winds up with an average of, say, .300 on the nose. Take away those hits and he's a mere .270 hitter.

In 1975, a young Ken Griffey Sr. garnered 38 infield hits for the Big Red Machine. He hit .305 on 141 total hits over 463 at-bats. If you took away those infield hits, many of which came on his sheer speed alone, and assumed all those bang-bang plays went against him, his average would have sunk to .242.

Griffey Sr. played on all grass surfaces in the minors, but knew that his game was predicated on speed. "My game was bunting," he said. "But when I got to the big leagues, my game was making good contact and hitting the ball on the ground and running because of the Astroturf. So I had to change my game completely."

A few other more recent examples: (1) When Kenny Lofton, who could motor down the line in a crisp 3.1 seconds, was 25 years old, he collected an eye-popping 31 hits on bunts. (2) In 2002 Juan Pierre led the majors with 55 infield hits (24 on bunts), two more than Ichiro accumulated that year. As was the case with the Griffey example, if Pierre had had no infield hits that year, he would have lost almost 100 points off his batting average and would have hit a pitiful .194 instead of .287! (3) Otis Nixon, in 1993, racked up 39 infield hits.

As Lofton once said, "I'm not a power hitter, so I must use speed to my advantage. You can't teach speed; either you have it or you don't." He also spoke of how his speed turned singles into doubles and doubles into three-base hits. The moment he hits the ball, his mind and legs begin to race. "First, I think about where I hit the ball," he began, "and [whether it is] still rolling when I hit first base. Then a lot of my decision to try for second depends on how I feel running that day."

A fine hitter, Torre was the antithesis of the greyhounds. He had to feel frustration when he'd hit the ball in, say, the hole deep at short only to get thrown out by an eyelash. In 1971, his greatest season, he lamented, "I didn't get any infield hits."

Lack of speed cost Cleveland great Al Rosen a Triple Crown. On the final day of the 1953 season he needed a hit in his last at-bat to top Washington's Mickey Vernon for the batting title. He was called out at first, even though the call could have easily gone either way. Rosen recalled, "I don't think I beat out an infield hit in my life. But everybody said I was safe on that one." He wound up with 43 homers and 145 RBIs to lead the league, but his .336 was one point less than Vernon's batting average.

One way for a player to help his batting average is simple: always hustle. After hitting a routine grounder, a hitter ideally should bust it down the line. One never knows—the ball might take a funny hop, and, even if the defense recovers, the hustling batter might get an infield hit.

Griffey Jr. once said that it's impossible for a player to hustle all the time during the long season. He said that on routine grounders he sometimes conserves energy by not going full speed. However, Fryman said, "I disagree a little bit. I think you play hard all the time. I think, probably what Ken is suggesting is it's really not possible to go 110 percent, to use that adage, all the time. You play at a very high level—what percentage, I don't know, but you're hustling all the time. But you're not going wide open all the time because you can't physically do that on a daily basis."

He said that in football "you hype up for six days to elevate yourself emotionally and physically to play one game. Baseball—we play everyday for such a long period of time—it requires a certain mentality of pacing yourself. So, you play at an elevated level. But, again, it's not wide open everyday. It's just not possible to do that."

Eddie Mathews's viewpoint was unequivocal. He used to say that he certainly didn't think it was asking too much for a player to make the effort to run hard down the line—a mere 90 feet—four times a day.

Burks commented, "You're going to have guys who have the God-given ability and the talent, but it does take hard work. I don't care how good you are, if you don't work hard, you're not going to polish it and you're not going to get any better."

Jason Varitek of the Boston Red Sox, a 2003 All-Star catcher, said that while great hand-eye coordination is obviously necessary to hit in the majors, it's also a given. Hard work is necessary, but is far from a given. "All major-league baseball players have the hand-eye coordination," he said. Therefore, all players, even the great ones, still need to put in the hard work.

Even the position a player takes on defense can, in some cases, influence his hitting. Traditionally, catchers, who spend so much time working on, thinking about, and even worrying about the defensive side of the game, hit for lower averages than players at positions such as first base.

During games catchers seldom have time to think about their hitting, as they're immersed in the details of how to work with their pitcher to defeat the opponent.

Finally, there's the importance of hitting left-handed, which is often a colossal advantage. After hitting the ball, lefties leave the box quicker, with their momentum carrying them towards first, and are about two steps closer to first than right-handers to begin with. That can make a difference in a game where many plays at first are photo finishes.

Further, since far more pitchers are right-handed, lefties have an edge in that they see the ball (e.g., on curves) coming toward them out of the hands of righties. All in all, left-handed hitters are more comfortable against the legion of righties they face than a right-handed hitter is.

The only awkward confrontation lefties face is that of lefty-on-lefty. However, frequently lefties avoid this match-up as either they are platooned or, especially against a tough southpaw such as Randy Johnson, they are given a day off. Right-handed hitters don't get as many chances growing up to face portside pitchers, so they don't gain the experience and comfort facing them that a lefty has against an opposite-throwing pitcher.

About 10 percent of Americans are left-handed. Accordingly, it would make sense that the percentage of lefties who do anything in any walk of life would also be around 10. However, a survey taken around 1990 revealed that about 25 percent of all hitters bat lefty. Not only that, of the 24 players who had hit .333 or better for a career, 16 were lefties, a remarkable 67 percent. Further, almost half the batters who have compiled 3,000 career hits are left-handed.

The same advantage holds true for power hitters. When Sammy Sosa and Rafael Palmeiro joined the 500-home-run club in early 2003, there were 19 players in that elite group. Not counting switch hitters, 8 of the 17 sluggers were lefties; that works out to 47 percent of them. Ken Griffey Jr. and Fred McGriff, both of whom are likely to reach the 500-homer plateau in 2004, are also left-handed batters. And, remarkably, four of the top five leaders in runs batted in are left-handed.

Bibliography

Books

Allen, Bob. *The 500 Home Run Club*. Champaign, Ill.: Sports Publications, 1999.

Berra, Yogi. *What Time is It? You Mean Now?* Waterville, Maine: Thorndike Press, 2003.

Cairns, Bob. *Pen Men*. New York: St. Martin's Press, 1992.

Carew, Rod. *Art and Science of Hitting*. New York: Penguin Books, 1986.

Davis, Hank. *Small Town Heroes*. Iowa City: University of Iowa Press, 1997.

Dickson, Paul. *Baseball's Greatest Quotations*. New York: Harper Perennial, 1991.

Gwynn, Tony. *The Art of Hitting*. New York: GT Publications, 1998.

Kindall, Jerry. *Science of Coaching Baseball*. Champaign, Ill.: Leisure Press, 1992.

Koppett, Leonard. *Thinking Man's Guide to Baseball*. New York: Dutton, 1967.

Lau, Charlie. *The Art of Hitting .300*. New York: Hawthorn Books, 1980.

Leonard, Bernardo. *The Superstar Hitter's Bible*. Lincolnwood, Ill.: Contemporary Books, 1998.

Ripken, Sr., Cal. *The Ripken Way*. New York: Pocket Books, 1999.

Rose, Pete. *Pete Rose on Hitting*. New York: Perigee Books, 1985.

Rosen, Ira. *Blue Skies Green Fields*. New York: Clarkson Potter, 2001.

Schmidt, Mike. *The Mike Schmidt Study*. Atlanta: McGriff & Bell, 1994.

Stewart, Wayne. *Indians on the Game*. Cleveland: Gray & Co., 2001.

————. *Fathers, Sons, and Baseball*. Guilford, Ct.: Lyons Press, 2002.

Williams, Ted. *The Science of Hitting*. New York: Simon & Schuster, 1986.

Periodicals

Arizona Fall League 2002 Program

Baseball Digest

Cleveland Plain Dealer

Cubs Quarterly

Elyria Chronicle-Telegram

The Gazette

Orange County Register

San Diego Union-Tribune

The Sporting News

Sports Illustrated

USA Today/Baseball Weekly

Index

About the Author

WAYNE STEWART WAS born and raised in Donora, Pennsylvania, a town that has produced several big-league baseball players, including Stan Musial and the Griffeys—father and son.

Mr. Stewart now lives in Lorain, Ohio, married to Nancy (Panich) Stewart. They have two sons, Sean and Scott.

Mr. Stewart has covered the baseball world as a writer for over 25 years, beginning in 1978. He has interviewed and profiled many Hall of Famers, such as Nolan Ryan, Bob Gibson, Robin Yount, Gaylord Perry, Warren Spahn, and Willie Stargell, as well as probable future Hall of Famers Joe Torre, Tony Gwynn, Greg Maddux, Rickey Henderson, Mike Schmidt, Frank Thomas, and Ken Griffey Jr. He has also interviewed or written stories on some of the biggest names in other sports, including Kareem Abdul-Jabbar, Larry Bird, and Jim Brown.

He has written seventeen baseball books to date, including *Baseball Oddities, Baseball Bafflers, Baseball Puzzlers, Indians on the Game, Fathers, Sons, and Baseball*, and 10 juvenile baseball books featuring the history of 10 big-league franchises. His works have also appeared in several baseball anthologies.

In addition, he has authored nearly 700 articles for national publications such as *Baseball Digest, USA Today/Baseball Weekly, Boys' Life*, and Beckett Publications. He has also written for the official team publications of many major-league clubs, such as the Braves, Yankees, White Sox, Orioles, Padres, Twins, Phillies, Red Sox, A's, and Dodgers.

Mr. Stewart has appeared on Cleveland's Fox 8 as a baseball expert and historian and on an ESPN Classic television show on Bob Feller. He also hosted his own radio shows on a small station in Lorain—a call-in, sports talk show; a pregame Indians report; pregame Notre Dame shows; and broadcasts of local baseball contests.